THE SHAPE OF THE CHURCH TO COME

THE SHAPE OF
THE CHURCH TO COME

Karl Rahner

TRANSLATION AND
INTRODUCTION BY
EDWARD QUINN

A Crossroad Book
THE SEABURY PRESS · New York

The Seabury Press
815 Second Avenue
New York, N.Y. 10017

First published in German with the title
Strukturwandel der Kirche als Aufgabe und
Chance, 1972
by Verlag Herder, Freiburg-im-Breisgau
© Karl Rahner, s.j. 1972
© Translation, S.P.C.K., 1974

Printed in the United States of America

LIBRARY OF CONGRESS CATALOGING IN
PUBLICATION DATA

Rahner, Karl, 1904–
  The shape of the church to come.

  "A Crossroad book."
  1. Church. I. Title.
BV600.2.R3613 1974   260   73–17907
ISBN 0–8164–1181–6

CONTENTS

INTRODUCTION

KARL RAHNER'S VISION

Karl Rahner is regarded as a difficult theologian. He is, in the same way that St Paul is difficult. He is at pains to bring home the mystery of salvation to twentieth-century man, to perform the theologian's true task of making faith blazingly intelligible first to himself and then to others. He is a Jesuit who brings out more than most of his contemporaries the meaning of the Dominican motto: *contemplata tradere*. He hands on gladly the fruits of his contemplation, a contemplation which has more to do with Jacob's wrestling with God than with Plato's vision of a world of ideas.

This may not be at first apparent when we find him using terms that may baffle even theologians, familiar with an older system: God as the quasi-formal cause of grace, the priority of uncreated grace, the 'supernatural existential'. But in the never-ending process of theological development—which should mean a deepening and ever-increasing joy in faith—these terms are necessary to get away from the abstract idea of two separate worlds, the one natural, the other supernatural; the one created by God as author of nature, the other from which God at an infinitely remote distance dispensed grace as an efficient cause analogous to if not entirely the same as a slot machine. Of course the old theology was never as crude as this, but in the hands of some of its less expert practitioners and in the mind of many a seminary student this was what it seemed to mean.

He is saying in sober and often highly complex prose what that other Jesuit, Gerard Manley Hopkins, had to say in poetry:

The world is charged with the grandeur of God

Nature and grace are distinct of course, but interwoven from the beginning in an eternal and indestructible pattern. God wills all men to be saved and his will cannot be without effect. Whether known or not, he is there personally in every nook and cranny of our world and at man's deepest roots, forming and shaping things to reflect back his glory. This is uncreated grace, not abstract but personal and concrete: so personal that the whole initiative in the single sweep of creation and salvation is the Father's; the Son, because he is Son, is incarnate and redeemer (abstract speculations about the possibility of any one of the Trinity becoming man are swept aside); and the world until transfigured by the Spirit and wholly restored by the Son to the Father is renewed little by little by that energy in man which we call created grace, always under the sway of the Spirit. Again in Hopkins' words:

> There lives the dearest freshness deep down things
> . . . .
> Because the Holy Ghost over the bent
> World broods . . .

What has this to do with the German synod? Everything. The whole work of the Church is this constant renewal of the earth and man under the guidance and with the power of the Holy Spirit, as an unceasing imitation and following of Christ, united with him in seeking and obeying his Father's will. The synod of the Catholic Church in Germany is part of that continual work of the Church.

It was a failure to appreciate these things which brought Professor Heinrich Flatten, a canonist, into conflict with Karl Rahner at the very opening of the synod in January 1971. Flatten attacked certain (unnamed) theologians, quoting and supporting Cardinal Höffner of Cologne who had said that some truths must be presupposed before any discussions at the synod, since to deny them was to be outside the Catholic faith: namely, Christ's divine sonship and resurrection, the Virgin Birth, the indissolubility of a consummated and validly contracted marriage. Rahner suggested that these unexceptionable assertions in this form were of little use to people today and could only be the occasion for further questioning and discussion, to some extent on the part of those Catholics who were most capable of making a contribution to the work of the synod.

Cardinal Höffner replied to Rahner in a friendly spirit, but insisting again on these indisputable presuppositions.* And again

---

* A translation of the correspondence was published in *The Month* (London, April 1971).

Rahner patiently pointed out that modern men, including devout and intelligent Catholics, will still ask just what is meant by saying 'Jesus is God': many Christians 'accept it while meaning something that is basically opposed to Church teaching'. As for indissoluble matrimony, the statement leaves a host of questions unanswered. The very meaning of the Gospel texts on this subject is not absolutely clear and settled for all time; the practice of the early Church and of the Eastern Churches today is not wholly irrelevant to our situation; the Pauline and the Petrine privileges do not necessarily exhaust the possibilities of dissolving an existing marriage; dissoluble or indissoluble, 'has someone before God no further moral right to marriage, simply because he cannot prove before the Church the real nullity of his former "marriage"?'

This book in a way continues the debate. The synod started without a basic concept to establish its aims, concentrate its activities, and provide a strategy for building up the Church of the future. The concept cannot be derived simply from unquestionable statements of faith, not even from the decrees of Vatican II. Theology even pastoral theology as taught until recently in the seminaries, cannot provide the concept. It has to be worked out in the light of all these, of the developments which are still continuing in all the sciences, of the constantly changing situation, above all of a world in between that settled, obedient world with which leading churchmen deal brilliantly and successfully and that which they say is rushing to disaster. Rahner has no intention of providing the basic concept—which would be too much to expect of any single individual or even of a single group—but only to put forward some preliminary considerations largely concerned with this very real and tangible world 'in between'. He is primarily interested in the Roman Catholic Church in Germany, but most of what he says holds for that Church in other Western countries and much of it for the other leading Churches in the West.

He asks us first to face the facts. Older people among us still remember and perhaps cling to a Church, established in fact if not in law, which simply provided for the spiritual needs of the same people as those who looked to the state and local authorities for the satisfaction of their temporal needs. This situation no longer holds and Christians cannot expect to find unquestioning support either in law or public opinion even for what were once universally accepted principles. They must expect to be 'a little flock', not retreating to a ghetto-like existence away from a world sunk in wickedness, but composed of those few who commit themselves with a living faith in Christ to the work of redeeming the world and rely solely on his grace to achieve this. This is the general trend, but we have to reckon with diversities in the transitional stage: drawing on the resources of the faith that really sustained the Church even when it seemed most firmly supported by society at large, curbing the violence of those who would uproot even the foundations of that faith. This means also upholding pluralism while rejecting polarization.

Rahner makes a number of quite startling suggestions for the future, but his very boldness arises from his sure theology and his perception of the facts. The authority of the Church, the *magisterium*, remains. But it must be much more careful to show that its teaching is rooted in the gospel and not expect people simply to accept the message just because it is given out by authority. The precise force of the teaching must be very clearly stated and the Church must be ready both to abandon positions which were no part of her essential claims and to put forward directives which are not asserted to be directly inspired by the Holy Spirit. The priest retains his important place, but he must work more and more in a declericalized Church, where all except the very limited functions which are his alone may well be exercised by others. He need not be celibate if the right choice for a particular congregation at a particular time would be a leader who is married or free to marry. It is not impossible that women may be ordained in a society where this is acceptable, since it cannot be shown that they were excluded from the priesthood in the past for other than sociological reasons.

He is particularly interesting on ecumenism. If we seriously want to bring about a unification of the Churches, we simply cannot wait until we have ironed out all doctrinal differences. Nor should we try to include in a united Church every possible type of Christian. But why should we not try even now to agree on a form of *institutional* unity between the major Churches of Christendom and look forward to a closer unity on doctrine as a result of this? This should be all the easier because there is already a much closer unity of outlook between practising Christians than denominational statements of faith might suggest. Not that there are so many declarations of this kind. Even the doctrines on which the Roman Catholic Church stands firm and immovable are largely those which are the common heritage of Christendom. Where differences occur, it is hard to see how they can be resolved quickly, if only because in the other Churches there is not an authority analogous to the Roman *magisterium* which can decide that certain teaching must be accepted or rejected. Of course the question must be raised as to the place of the Pope in this institutional unity. Here it would seem that Protestants not only reject the Vatican dogma, but also its practical consequences. Rahner appeals to them to accept the papacy precisely in the form that most of them accept it anyway: as a Petrine ministry which would remain in the united Church as a leadership no more obtrusive than that which the Pope exercises when he appeals to the United Nations or calls Christians to prayer and to the practice of their religion in accordance with their denominational traditions. Roman Catholics would continue to accept within their own area of such a united Church a more exclusive and far-reaching authority.

Finally, Rahner's recommendation of 'basic communities' (*Basis-gemeinden*)* may puzzle many people and seem too much in the air for practically minded parish priests. But there is no question of 'inventing' these or discarding forthwith the existing parochial structures. To some extent they already exist (in university chaplaincies, for instance, where the congregation is composed to a far greater extent than elsewhere of people who are freely committed to much more than a perfunctory attendance at Sunday Mass) and parishes will continue to be essential and important in the life of the Church to the extent that they are filled with Christians who find there the radiant centre from which they spread the good news of the gospel and go out to serve their neighbours in practical works of love. But it is unlikely that churches filled with people who come out of habit, simply because they were brought up that way, will continue

---

* This term is used to signify those church communities which have built themselves up through free and spontaneous initiative, in contrast to institutionalized church structures, such as parishes having a legal and geographical basis.

much longer. We shall have to reckon with far smaller numbers, but with more active missionary-minded members: 'It means more to win one new Christian from what we may call neo-paganism than to keep ten "old Christians".' A hard saying? Not if we understand rightly what was implicit in the 'old theology' and what Rahner has developed more explicitly: the effective saving will of God outside the boundaries of the visible Church and the sacraments.

Even if we put all our heart into building up this 'Church from the roots', but without forgetting the ardent faith which made the older Church infinitely more than a place of refuge for our private spiritual needs, it is still true that 'God's strategy of salvation and that of the Church are not simply identical'.

EDWARD QUINN

AUTHOR'S PREFACE

The theme of this little book is clear from its title and from what I have to say in the first pages. For the moment, no more need be said about this. I hand the book over to the reader without knowing how it will fare. Many perhaps will feel that it is too 'progressive' and (ecclesiastically) too much to the 'left', but others may consider it altogether too conservative. Many will say that I too don't know the future of the Church, although I am talking about it. And in this respect they are right, for I am not a prophet and the Church's future is ultimately an object of hoping against hope and not a matter of futurology. Others will say that the selection of themes is arbitrary and has not turned out well. How can this be disproved? Anyone who criticizes in this way however must permit us to ask how he thinks a more exact selection of topics should be made and why his selection is absolutely right. I would be very interested in his answer.

It is clear that the topics are restricted to those questions which seem most urgent in our situation in Germany. I am of course aware that the problems have not been cleared up simply by this book; they need to be considered also by many other theologians, Christians, and churchmen. Only in this way can the Church develop slowly but clearly a collective conscious-ness of the basic conceptions which must today guide her action for the future, so that individual decisions can be appropriately harmonized up to a point and therefore that we don't simply 'carry on' as we have been doing, when foresight and planning are possible for the Christian and indeed required of him.

KARL RAHNER

THE SYNOD'S PROBLEMS

The Spirit of God, faith, hope, and love shown in living deeds, will decide the fate of the German Church in the next decades far more than all the resolutions of the synod, however good we are hoping these will be; and, if they are not to remain merely on paper, the Spirit of God himself will have to endow them all with the spirit and life of the Church. Nevertheless the synod is or—better—ought to become an important event in the history of the German Church. But this is possible only if we enter on the tasks which the synod puts before us with all the powers of mind and heart at our command.

It seems to me, however (I hope my fears are groundless), that the members of the synod have plunged into individual questions *as* individual at once with such eagerness that they may fail to grasp clearly enough the task before them as a single whole. Up to now the *praesidium** of the synod and its central committee have set to work mainly on purely legal formalities and problems of organization. The synod may at best have become marginally aware of a really clear basic plan for its task as a single whole, as a result of the committee at least beginning to consider how many and just which particular proposals can seriously be brought forward for discussion, what is the maximum period of time available, and thus the range of subjects to be discussed. As far as I know, each of the special commissions turned at once to the mass of the questions assigned to it, completed work on particular proposals, or at least set to work on them, without ever raising precisely the question of the place and relative value which the themes assigned can and ought to have within a total concept of the synod. This basic conception has therefore hitherto remained obscure. This to a large extent is due to the fact that the task of the synod as indicated in its statute is too general and too much taken for

* The German term has been retained, since the particular presiding body active at the synod is meant.

granted for anyone to assume that he really knows what the synod has to do, merely by repeating the words.

The list of themes drawn up by the second preparatory commission before the beginning of the synod in January 1971 and intended to be a guide for the special commissions contains indeed a lot of quite good material, but so much of it that—if you will pardon the expression—you can't see the wood for the trees. It offers no criterion of selection from an almost endless list of themes. It might have been thought that the investigation of such a basic understanding of the synod would be the function of the first of the special commissions. But, apart from the fact that this commission too was assigned a mass of individual questions which could and did claim fully its working resources, the question of the single meaning and single task of the synod in the light of its basic conception, overriding everything else, was at least not raised in fact nor answered even by this commission.

But can the synod get through without such a basic concept? Driven by the thousands of needs in the ordinary life of the Church today, can it simply throw itself at once into the midst of the work on individual questions without knowing which are the most urgent? Without knowing what must be the basic trend of the answers? Without knowing on what principles the obligation to maintain a tradition and the necessity of creatively shaping the future can be reconciled with one another? To be perfectly honest (even though all comparisons are lame), I must say that the synod at the beginning of its first working session seemed to me like a parliament which has no government, doesn't choose one, or—if you like to regard the elected *praesidium* of the synod as a kind of government—has not received at the beginning any declaration of policy from the government. You may think that the comparison is too lame, but it is true that the synod at any rate up to now has not provided itself with any such basic concept (which cannot simply be taken for granted, but would have to be produced as the result of a decision taken after thorough discussion), has evidently no intention of doing so, and clearly does not possess an organ or instrument to find or decide on anything of the kind.

It cannot be said that such a basic concept is superfluous as an individual theme for its own sake, that what is meant by it is involved as inner activation in the discussions and resolutions on individual proposals and in fact can be worked out and discovered ultimately only from the material presented for discussion. Reflection therefore on this secret activation shaping all the individual proposals can at best come only at the end as a kind of supplement to the work of the synod.

There is a sense in which this may well be true, since the meaning and import of the ultimate principles behind the whole process can be known exactly only in their concrete application and operation. But this does not exclude or render superfluous a primary reflection at the beginning of the synod on the ultimate principles which must sustain the work on concrete questions. Otherwise there is a danger that the synod, without any real shape of its own, will split up into groups, each conducting its own business and then having the amorphous results of its work confirmed at the end by each of the other groups (called special commissions), the latter being ultimately uninterested in the work and resolutions of the rest and having no standards at all by which to judge the work of others and its results. The synod must have in mind a basic conception, a basic trend for its efforts, ultimate norms of selection for its work. Otherwise, at most, some good individual results may be expected from the synod; but the hope would have to be abandoned that the synod might in principle show to the German Church a way through the next decades and compel it by legally binding directives to proceed on this way and no other.

Nor finally can it be said that this basic conception is adequately provided by the Christian and Catholic faith that we all profess and by the declarations and decrees of the Second Vatican Council, which the synod intends to apply to German conditions. Obviously these two factors, which are binding on us, though in varying degrees, impose a certain framework within which the work and resolutions of the synod have to be kept and provide certain basic initiatives for its work. But this is far from clarifying that basic concept which is necessary for the synod.

For this, first of all, the Christian and Catholic faith is too general—quite apart from the fact that more concrete norms and laws, however much they have to correspond to this faith, cannot be and are not simply or always purely logical deductions from the principles of this faith; on the contrary they also always carry within themselves the uniqueness of the concretely historical factor and the free act by which they are set up. It is likewise obvious that the Second Vatican Council cannot dispense us from the work of asking about such a basic concept. This council has certainly a lasting importance for the Church as a whole and so too for the German Church, which (if we may put it in this way) ought not to be depreciated either from the Right or from the Left. But in the positive decisions of the council, if we look at them quite coolly, there is much that is already obsolete —in the decree on the liturgy, for example. Many of the council's statements simply express the Christian faith and that, often enough, in the light of presuppositions and horizons of understanding which cannot simply be regarded as those of today or tomorrow. And, in any event, the declarations of a council addressed to the whole Church are too general for us to be able to turn them at once and directly into individual norms. This great council doesn't make our task as simple as that.

We must draw attention to another aspect. In principle the synod has no aligned parties or groups. We may indeed get the impression that one such group exists: the bishops' conference, particularly since the latter has tried to create and maintain the impression of having a uniform opinion on all questions which it announces immediately at the opening of discussions on each individual proposal. But the bishops—we hope—will deny that they want to form a solid group at the synod. And it is to be hoped that this assurance will become clearer in the course of the synod than it has been hitherto. For it would indeed be odd if all the bishops were of one opinion in all individual questions, even those of slight importance. For if their opinion were *a priori* correct, the synod could be dissolved at once and all decisions could be left to the bishops. But if we assume that this uniform opinion is not necessarily right in regard to the matter under consideration, then it is surprising that it turns out to be so uniform.

We might ask if the reasons for this uniformity have perhaps nothing or very little to do with the matter in hand, whether in fact it is the will of a group which in every case and on every question seeks to act as a solid body, as a clique, and as a party. But then two things follow.

1 Such a solid group would have no reason to take offence if other members of the synod were also to join together in aligned groups for particular purposes, in order to make their opinion and trend effective, since it cannot be assumed that an opinion deviating from that of the bishops is *a priori* absurd and false.

2 It would be desirable for both the bishops' group and the other fundamentally legitimate groups to conceive and clearly state something like a programme of principles, so that people would know what principles were involved in individual decisions.

If we want to substantiate such individual decisions, it is evident that an appeal to our common faith, to the declarations of Vatican II, to the proximate objective reasons for an individual decision, is not adequate even for the understanding of an opinion on a particular question. If an individual develops something like such a programme of principles, he formulates first of all of course only his own opinion, particularly if he is not a bishop. But even a statement of this kind could perhaps encourage reflection with others on the desirable fundamental orientation of the synod in its individual decisions, could make clearer the basic attitudes—often not really thought out—from which these individual decisions emerge.

Of course it cannot be *my* intention or task here to give an account of such a basic concept together with the preliminary considerations on which it is based. Merely to present the outline of such a conception to the synod would far outstrip my competence. Indeed, even the attempt to produce an outline is beyond my resources, my experience and understanding of the religious and pastoral tasks of the Church in Germany today and tomorrow: a really adequate understanding of the intellectual and social situation today, in which and in the light of which such a basic conception must be drafted, is in fact beyond the powers of any single individual.

Such a basic concept, which could seriously command the freely given support of a broad majority in the Church, cannot be offered at all by an individual, unless he has behind him (which is not the case here) explicitly or at least factually a large group of those who make and carry out decisions. Nevertheless,

I think I ought at least to make a modest attempt to give an account of some preliminary considerations in regard to such a concept. If this sort of attempt were *a priori* meaningless or superfluous, how then could a basic concept—whether it is agreed or exists without a legal sanction of its own—come into existence at all? One must have the courage to adopt and also to profess an opinion on this matter. If latent differences of opinion become manifest at the synod as a result of the public expression of these reflections on a basic conception, and consequently 'parties' of a kind are formed, even if not in legal form, each professing a different basic concept, with different basic orientations, then this cannot be avoided: it only makes manifest what exists anyway, even though latent and suppressed, and therefore can be effective in a relevant and rational way only when it is honestly admitted and drawn into the consciousness of Church and synod.

If, then, what I would like to present as preliminary considerations on a basic concept for the synod were to be regarded by others as a kind of manifesto of a trend in the Church, of a 'party'—even though not aligned—at the synod, I would not *a priori* and in principle reject this description. Admittedly, everyone is bound to be as 'objective' and 'balanced' as possible in his reflections; everyone should expect others to agree only on such norms of behaviour as can rightly and seriously be required of them. But no one can in fact be simply and straightforwardly non-partisan. If a person acts as if he were neutral, he is only making a bad attempt to conceal the subjective limitations of his reflections and to impose them on others as something obvious and not in need of discussion. But this sort of thing is false and in our case therefore not suitable to the matter in hand, since it is a question of reflections preparatory to decisions inevitably based on discretionary judgements and even very often necessarily making a selection from possibilities which may seem equally to be justified in the light of purely rational consideration.

There are still some further observations to be made before beginning to reflect on a basic conception for the synod. These reflections are fragmentary: they must deal with the most varied things, so that one person alone cannot be an expert in all the particular disciplines which are concerned with these diverse realities. These reflections obviously cannot in themselves and alone bridge the gulf which undeniably exists between theoretical and practical reason. They are not prophecies by someone who thinks he knows already what only the next decades will bring. If some ideas seem Utopian to others, then all I can say is that even Utopias can be great historical forces, that they can throw a sudden and sharp light today on the possibilities of tomorrow, and that I myself rather regret that at my age weariness and resignation leave me incapable of saying *more* about Utopia for fear of sticking too little to the so-called solid basis of facts and real possibilities.

What I want to say here may conveniently be divided into three parts, corresponding to the three questions:

1 Where do we stand?

2 What are we to do?

3 How can the Church of the future be conceived?

For the time being, there is certainly no more to be said by way of justifying this division in principle, on the meaning of each question or on the sequence of the questions. For the sake of clarity, it should be noted that the second part deals with the more immediate future, its tasks and possibilities; the third part however looks forward to a more distant future.

PART ONE
Where do we stand?

1

ANALYSIS OF THE SITUATION

The question, 'Where do we stand?', is about the historical and social situation in which the Catholic Church is placed today in virtue of her environment, in which she must live and fulfil her mission, in the light of which, and in regard to which she must make her decisions. If all that the synod has to ask, to discuss, and to decide relates to pastoral care and is therefore material for pastoral theology, and if only the term 'pastoral theology' is understood precisely and comprehensively enough, then it is clear that a theological analysis of the situation must be expressly or tacitly the starting point of the synod's reflections. For pastoral theology must not remain confined within an abstract dogmatic and moral theology and the general principles derived from these, but must reflect in the light of these principles on the historical and social situation in which the Church is living and must live here and now. Without such an analysis of the situation, which the theologian can provide from his own principles and must not simply leave to the secular historical and social sciences (however much he must respect their conclusions and bring them into his own reflections), pastoral theology would be merely a part of dogmatic and moral theology, a medley of prescriptions based on the uncritically accepted 'experience' of its practitioners.

The same, however, holds also of a pastorally aligned synod, one therefore necessarily following the lead of pastoral theology. The synod, too, may not simply assume that everyone—and priests and bishops in particular—always knows from his own experience (most people find that this only confirms their preconceived opinions) the situation in which the Church is living today and in which and in regard to which she must carry out her mission. We need only listen critically particularly to churchmen, bishops, and priests, when they undertake to describe this situation as if it were the easiest thing in the world. The description is mostly (we gladly admit exceptions) made up of two parts: the description of a situation with which these men cope brilliantly, in which they do exactly what is required of them and do it successfully; and a description of a world in which faith and morality decline more and more and which people do little or nothing to withstand. The world, the real world *in between*, is mostly absent from such a description which stems from experience without reflection: the world presenting tasks which the churchmen are not yet fulfilling, which are really new but certainly provide opportunities for mastering them. Because people don't see *this* world clearly, their own awareness of the concrete Church very often becomes an odd mixture of a stubborn conservatism (we know indeed what we have to do and we do it very well) and an unadmitted despair. In a world in the process of evolution, offering less and less ground out of which a genuine Christianity could grow, things go more and more downhill, and we can neither understand why God should permit times so unfruitful for Christianity nor foresee any end to them. We can therefore only go on being depressed (this too is concealed and unadmitted), because we cannot 'get out' and yet—fortunately—don't have to expect the end in our own lifetime. A theologically worked out analysis of the situation should be before the synod from the beginning, whether the analysis is produced by the synod itself or carried out in advance elsewhere (but where?).

It would, of course, be absurd to attempt here from my own knowledge and on my own authority to produce a theological analysis of the situation or even merely expound one already available. But I must venture to make some observations on this theme. It doesn't matter at all to me if then historians of ideas, sociologists, and political theorists, sociologists of religion, show some sympathy or are irritated by my incompetence and ignorance or if others condescendingly observe that all I have said here is already well known and has been said better elsewhere. In these reflections on the question of where the German Church stands today and what her situation is, I am not concerned to distinguish very precisely between the simple description of the situation and the consequences for pastoral care and pastoral theology which directly flow from that description and which alone really throw light on the situation and therefore may also be touched on here.

Some well-known peculiar features of this situation of a general character and not merely relating to the sociology of religion may first of all be briefly enumerated, even though we cannot consider them thoroughly here in theological terms. We are living in a world in which the historical fields—formerly more or less separated culturally, socially and politically—have grown or are growing together into a unity. The result is that each has become everybody's neighbour, even though in varying degrees, and therefore also the 'foreign policy' of a 'regional Church' and her 'home policy' have and are bound to have such an influence on each other that one can scarcely be distinguished from the other. We are living in a world in which the general consciousness of society and of each individual is fundamentally and deeply stamped by the sciences, that is, by the historical sciences which, despite their function of summing up general trends, tend to make historical realities relative, by the autonomous, exact, and functional natural sciences and by the empirical social sciences thinking likewise almost in the same terms. Man's 'metaphysical' and religious consciousness can exist openly and have the chance of a future only by entering without hesitation into a symbiosis with this scientific consciousness and its sceptical rationality and by not placing God where the scientist with his own methods would be expected to find him but cannot.

We are living in an age of the mass society where authority is regarded as merely functional, and in which, by an odd juxtaposition, freedom and interdependence have become key-concepts and mutually both threaten and substantiate each other. We are living in a world in which man in the most diverse dimensions has become the object of his own power to manipulate and change. The result is that he can scarcely continue to regard himself as a finished image of God but sees himself rather as *the* point of the cosmos at which its journey, guided by Utopian plans, begins into the wholly undefined future. We are living in a world in which depth-psychology is discovering in man abysses which, on the one hand, it seeks to control, not through an appeal to the rational freedom of the subject, but through psychotechnics conceived in terms of natural science and, on the other hand, undertakes to resolve man into the anonymous forces of his biological and social origin. We are living in a world which is a society under the direction of the mass-media, where no one can know any longer who directs the media themselves. We are living in a world in which the ideal types, in the light of which man understands his own nature, have become mobile and plural, so that in any particular cultural sphere there is no longer an ideal accepted publicly and by everyone which the individual with good will can take for granted as that which he must strive to realize in himself. Finally, we are living in a world whose society is pluralistic: that is, in which, even in the individual historical spheres, there is no longer a society which sets up concrete guide-lines for all its groups.

To describe the religio-sociological situation of the Church in the light of this summary characterization, we would have to speak of what might be called the 'remnants' of the past. There are still considerable remnants of a socially constituted, traditional Christianity, a Christianity possessing a certain official status in society. This was formerly taken for granted as a social factor and therefore could be rejected only by an act of unbelief, which remained essentially private, or by a protest—which could be dangerous—against the homogeneous public opinion of society. Such remnants of traditional and socially constituted Christianity in this sense certainly still exist; we need not be ashamed of them, nor have we *a priori* in virtue of any sort of formally democratic principles the duty of demolishing them. But they *are* remnants and they are sustained by those other remnants of a secular historical period, which also persist to the present time and are, up to a point, effective in it. This former society was in fact in its secular culture also homogeneous, hierarchically structured, and with a common public opinion, which was prior to the individual's decision and shaping of his life in a much more unambiguous way than it is today. It is important therefore to see clearly that the formerly homogeneous Christian character of society as such was the result of and an element in the unity and homogeneousness of secular society, thus making it necessary for us to investigate what were the grounds and factors of this secular, social homogeneousness.

The homogeneous Christian character of our Western civilization throughout a thousand years was not the effect of a miracle of God's grace, external and additional to the intra-

mundane causes and elements of a secular-homogeneous culture
and society, nor was it really constituted by the free decision
of faith on the part of all individuals, which was directed to
the same end but could then be understood only as miraculous;
the homogeneous Christian character of that former culture
and society was simply of one piece with the homogeneousness
of secular culture and society.

For the men of that passing and largely past age, this can
certainly be interpreted theologically as grace, through which
God placed the decision of faith—necessary also for them—
before men in a particular form but without absolving them
from the necessity of making it. But we certainly no longer have
this grace in so far as we live and make our decision of faith
in the light of the special conditions of our own time and do
not live and act in the light of the remnants of a past age still
effective in our time.

We cannot rely on this 'grace' for today or for any foreseeable future, nor do we need to do so. The 'grace' is denied us
of a homogeneous Christian society which itself provides for all
strictly Christian patterns of behaviour and in this respect marks
out a place for the decision of Christian faith and in a certain
sense facilitates it. We need have no regrets for this external,
(in theological terms) 'medicinal' grace of faith, as it is more
and more withdrawn from us with the passing away of a
secular-homogeneous culture and society. For in a sense at least
it was contrary to the ultimate nature of faith, since the latter
means a decision for God and his call which in the last resort
must be made always in a critical dissociation from the 'world':
that is, from the current ways of thinking and behaviour in
the person's social environment.

The situation of Christians and thus of the Church today is
therefore one of transition from a people's Church,* corresponding to the former homogeneous, secular society and culture, to
a Church as that community of believers who critically dissociate
themselves, in virtue of a personal free decision in every case,
from the current opinions and feelings of their social environment, and who also find and imprint on properly theological

* There is no exact English equivalent for *Volkskirche*, which signifies
the Church of the country or area, providing for its spiritual needs, just
as the national or local government provides for its temporal needs.

faith its special character, perhaps precisely in and through a critical attitude to their society and its ruling forces. Against these, no fearful clinging to the remnants we have mentioned of a homogeneous secular and Christian society of former times is of any use; no return of the Church's missionary activity to the so-called 'little flock' is of any use, although this flock still exists among the remnants and thus presents an opportunity— constantly shrinking—for the Church to go on in the old style, until the very last bourgeois and rural oases from these remnants of an historical epoch, moving towards its end, will have more or less entirely disappeared.

This does not mean that it is forbidden—indeed, there is an obligation—to prevent by every means an over-rapid decline of whatever still exists and can be preserved of these remnants. It is of course always the Church's task to carry over that which remains forever and which has hitherto been authentically represented in these declining forms of a secular and religious culture and society, into a new form more appropriate to the present and future than the form now slowly but inevitably crumbling and thus to hand on this permanent reality authentically and effectively to the coming age.

None of this alters the fact that our present situation is one of transition from a Church sustained by a homogeneously Christian society and almost identical with it, from a people's Church, to a Church made up of those who have struggled against their environment in order to reach a personally clearly and explicitly responsible decision of faith. This will be the Church of the future or there will be no Church at all. But we believe in the permanence of the Church in the world and history, and hope for this permanence also for the history of *our* people; nevertheless we have to strive for the greatest possible number of members of the Church and thus cannot be content to set our hopes on a little heap called Church, trusting to be sheltered from the winds in history and society. That is why the clear, frank and bold acceptance of the situation is a basic question for the Church today and for the synod.

What concrete conclusions are to be drawn from all this for the German Church's self-understanding must be considered at greater length later. Here we must, first of all, clearly visualize the situation itself. The often lamented decline of Christian ways and faith is not the work or effect of sinister forces nor even primarily a decline of really necessary, saving faith (whether and to what extent there is such a thing, we can never know). It is simply the disappearance of the preconditions of that very special kind of faith and Christianity, by no means identical with the essence of faith and Christianity, which was involved in social conditions which are now disappearing and could not be assumed as permanent by Christian faith, since they are not at all necessary for a true and ecclesial Christianity.

This transitional state might be described more precisely than is possible here. To characterize the situation, we should have to include all those special features which we first briefly summarized. Then we would have to show that Christianity and the Church today, and still more tomorrow, will be living in a situation in which the general and public consciousness, marked by the empirical sciences and their methods, knows no world in which God occurs as one particular reality among others, but only a world which, although not really excluding faith and all reference to God, is in a quite definite sense a-theistic. It would have to be shown that this situation forbids all religious institutional forms to assume a sacral aura, to be invested with a kind of taboo, in regard to which opposition and indifference would be bound to seem *a priori* reprehensible and socially offensive. It would have to be made clearer that the situation *either* in the long run leads to an a-religious attitude, no longer faced with the alternative of belief or unbelief, *or* it demands from the individual and from the ecclesial society a constantly new formation of faith from its ultimate sources: a faith which can no longer rely on the support of its objective expressions already existing and socially accepted and therefore faces many of these secondary objective expressions of a theological, ritual and ecclesial-institutional character with a rather more non-committal attitude than at the time when these had an indisputable status in society. We should have to distinguish this situation by the fact that personal and representational authorities (office, office-holders, Scripture, Christian-ecclesial celebration of particular events in life by infant baptism, first communion, Christian burial, etc.) become credible only when, on the one hand, they are constantly substantiated afresh in the light of the ultimate experiences of life and of God and at the same time exercise a beneficial influence on ordinary people in an empirically palpable and really intelligible fashion.

We are living also in a situation in which the universal history of religion is better known and therefore historical revelation as the justification of faith can no longer be understood so easily as it was formerly, spontaneously and naïvely, as a regionally and temporally limited event in history. But this situation of the Church and of faith may have existed formerly as the situation of particular individuals; today it has become general, a situation of society as such affecting every individual, although varying in the form and intensity of its influence.

The description of the situation of the German Church could certainly be extended and deepened in many respects. But it seems to me even so significant enough. The real consequences of this transitional state must be considered more closely later. This sketchy characterization of our situation might seem too obvious or too barren if we did not point out that those who hold office and the good, zealous Christians in our Church are generally unwilling to admit this transitional state to a sufficient extent. The basic tendency with us is to defend what has been handed down, not to prepare for a situation which is still to come. Indeed, it is often said that the function of authority is primarily to defend things as they exist and to leave to other forces in the Church what is to come, what is new, to be creatively shaped.

This may be right as a description of what exists in fact. The office-holders, who are obviously limited and sinful men and simply cannot avoid being influenced by this fact in exercising their office, will only too readily defend things as they are because they are thereby also justifying and defending themselves. But, together with their necessary function of defending the traditional, office-holders in the Church as such have at least equally the right and the sacred duty to provide for the Church's endurance in a situation still to come. Are these office-holders and the pious Christians who are only too ready to be identified with them sufficiently aware of this equally—if not more—important task of preparation for the future? When something new is suggested and required, don't they first ask almost instinctively whether and how this is compatible with existing practice and tradition? Does not an at least equally urgent question very often occur to them much too late or in too mild a form? Whether the new is not required by the situation now emerging or to be taken for granted in it?

If we imagine the situation as it may well be in ten years or even earlier, shall we not be glad to see that 'laymen' are still present at Mass and get up to speak there? Do we have then to treat the problem of 'lay-preaching' with so many 'ifs' and 'buts', with so much theological misgiving ultimately irrelevant to the future situation? Does not the same hold for the juridical structures of a parish or a diocese? Will not any bishop or parish priest soon be delighted whenever laypeople take on even the least share of responsibility? When we examine the orthodoxy of a new statement of the Christian faith, do we at the same time think equally quickly and with the same concentration of how the Christian faith must be proclaimed when it is no longer propped up by prevailing social realities? In such questions of orthodoxy do we not assume too often and too quickly that what is customary is perfectly clear and orthodox? Would we not cease to take these things for granted if we were to place ourselves in the situation of the Christians of tomorrow (who exist anyway in considerable numbers today)? I would be interested to see the reaction of the majority of the bishops and other members of the synod if perhaps some diffident attempts are made to formulate the old faith and the old hope in a way which will also be acceptable tomorrow.

In such a transitional state, between a people's Church and a Church of those who believe clearly as a result of their own decision, the traditional in virtue of its familiarity and persistence in former times (but, to be exact, only in those times) will always seem more convincing than the new and untried. But if we honestly admit that we are in a period of transition, if we are convinced that what is to remain of the old can be salvaged only by being resolutely accepted as we accept the new situation, must we—and particularly authority—not think more of the future than of the present and past? Must we not adopt a spirit of self-criticism and resist a very dubious conservatism, which is becoming virulent as the euphoria of Vatican II is fading and the ordinary routine begins again, when we must set to work seriously and some confusion cannot be avoided?

We shall have to return constantly to this situation when

answering our second and third questions. Hence, while we are still occupied with the first, the description already given of the situation may be sufficient even though it is very rough and based on a somewhat arbitrary selection of facts.

2

CHURCH OF THE LITTLE FLOCK

To answer the question, Where do we stand?, a mere analysis of the situation of the German Church will not suffice: something must be said of the German Church itself.

In attempting to answer this further question, we are not going to reproduce a dogmatic treatise on ecclesiology, applying to the German Church all that is said there of the Church in general, on the ground that the Church as such is present and becomes an historical event in this as in every regional Church. We are assuming here that this traditional ecclesiology is known and acceptable.

At the same time we are well aware of the problems created by taking for granted the ultimate, fundamental propositions on the Church. But it is only by presupposing this basic ecclesiology—which concretely and practically is by no means obvious—that our remarks can be correctly understood and appreciated at their true, but not necessarily the highest value.

We have to speak therefore of the German Church only in so far as it is affected by the situation in which it is living and which we briefly outlined.

We are the beginning of the little flock. I say 'the beginning' because, without being really deeply disturbed in my faith, I am sure that in the next decades the German Church will decline quite considerably numerically, at least in relation to the total population, and in social influence. Christian and ecclesially institutionalized faith will also weaken considerably, even though it is not yet by any means possible to judge categorically whether the relation between *the* faith and *the* unbelief which *ultimately* decide a person's final salvation will be very much altered in our time and in our future.

But when we speak of ourselves today as the beginning of the little flock, we must first remove a misunderstanding. 'Little flock' does not mean the same as ghetto or sect, since these are defined not by numbers but by a mentality: a mentality which the Church can afford in the future even less than today, no matter how large or small the numbers in the German Church may be or become. Where a sectarian or ghetto mentality is propagated among us—not of course under this label, but in fact—under the pretext that we are or are becoming Christ's little flock which has to profess the folly of faith and of the cross, it must be fought with the utmost severity in the name of true faith and authentic Christianity. If we talk of the 'little flock' to defend our cosy traditionalism and stale pseudo-orthodoxy, in fear of the mentality of modern man and modern society, if we tacitly consent to the departure of restless, questioning people from the Church, so that we can return to our repose and orderly life and everything in the Church becomes as it was before, we are propagating, not the attitude proper to Christ's little flock, but a petty sectarian mentality. This is all the more dangerous because it shows up, not under its true name, but in an appeal to orthodoxy, church-loyalty and strict morality.

The smaller Christ's flock becomes in the pluralism of modern society, so much the less can it afford a mentality of the ghetto and the sect, so much more open must it be to the outer world, so much more precisely and boldly must it ask in every given case where the frontiers really lie between the Church and an unbelieving world. They certainly do not lie where a diehard cosy traditionalism wants to place them in the most diverse areas of the Church.

Assuming all this and taking it quite seriously, it must nevertheless be said that, by any human estimate, the Church in Germany will become numerically smaller, particularly by comparison with the total population. This prospect, which must be frankly and boldly recognized, does not refer merely to the number of 'practising' Catholics who really take part in the life of the Church. However unpleasant it may be, we must also allow for the fact that social conditions in the long or short run may be so transformed (whatever the cause of this may be) that civic respectability and normality will no longer require a person to be a baptized Christian, to pay church-tax, or send his children to denominational religious instruction, to add a religious touch to marriages and funerals, that it will soon be no longer socially out of place or damaging to withdraw officially from the Church. A development of this kind in the more immediate future need not be caused by any striking political upheavals; in our modern society there are plenty of causes leading slowly and unobtrusively to such a situation, so that only a single occasion—perhaps insignificant in itself—is necessary to let loose a rapid and numerically very great falling away from the Church. In any case we cannot for much longer expect the core of practising churchpeople to be surrounded and secured by a large number of those who must still officially be called Christian, giving us a false confidence even today when we speak of a Christian society.

This society no longer exists, however fluid the transitions may be between the real Christians and the nominal Christians, however many chances there still may be to win back relatively easily such nominal Christians, however great may be the chance of the Church in Germany even in the future still to retain with courage and confidence a relatively large number of real Christians through her traditional methods of transmitting the faith or to win them back by new missionary methods. We are a little flock in society and we shall become a much smaller flock, since the erosion of the preconditions of a Christian society within the secular society still continues and thus takes away the ground more and more from a traditional Christianity.

The real question resulting from this is more or less: What must the Church do in view of this situation and the foreseeable further development? Certainly there is no reason for a bigoted and pharasaic lamentation on the faithlessness of the world or for a desperate expectation that the last day will soon dawn. There is however reason to ask where and how the Church in her actual life and action was and still is herself the cause of the decline of an explicitly ecclesial Christianity. Is this the result of an old-fashioned theology and proclamation, of a lifestyle on the part of office-holders and other Christians which makes Christianity look historically obsolete, and so on? Much will have to be said about these things in other connections, so that for the moment we can be content with this general reference.

We must, however, draw attention to a quite essential and fundamental consequence of this situation of the Church as a dwindling flock. The Church in her proclamation and in her life must insist on an aggressive attitude in all situations to win

new Christians from an 'unchristian' milieu and not be content
with merely defending her traditional substance. This principle
seems to me clear and intelligible in itself if only we remember
that the real causes of the traditionally homogeneous Christianity in society do not lie at all in the Church's power, in
grace and in men's goodwill, but are of a secular nature, so that
even the remnants of such a traditional Christianity cannot be
saved by means directly at the disposal of the Church or be
activated by an appeal to bold faith and missionary zeal.

Someone might object that faith and Christian life were
transmitted even in former times not simply through the mere
existence of a secular, homogeneous society, but through active
faith, proclamation, and convincing, genuine, living example.
All this is obviously true and important, but—rightly understood
—proves the very thing we have just formulated as the basic
principle in the Church's missionary strategy. For if bold faith,
living proclamation, and the example of a genuine Christian
life, can produce Christians, then, if these causes are correctly
worked out—that is, adapted to the situation—and applied,
they must also be able to win *new* Christians from an unchristian
milieu. Anyone who denies this, expressly or merely in practice,
surreptitiously, is really saying that the transmission of Christianity in the last centuries was a secular, historical and social
phenomenon and nothing more. The possibility therefore of
winning new Christians from a milieu that has become unchristian is the sole living and convincing evidence that even
today Christianity still has a real chance for the future. The
attempt merely to defend the remnants of a traditional Christianity would inevitably conceal from us the true causes of
an avoidable decline of Christianity among ourselves, since we
would then simply go on in the old way, which in fact is adapted to the preservation of the old Christianity, and we would
therefore by no means be forced to open our minds to new
ideas for missionary activity.

So there we are. It means more to win one new Christian
from what we may call neopaganism than to keep ten 'old
Christians'. Even though it seems to aim at numerically slight
results, even if at first perhaps it produces from these 'neopagans' only people who are interested in Christianity and the
Church, the missionary offensive is the only method of defence

which promises success in preserving the old remnant of the past of Western Christianity. Only in this way can people even in the remnant get rid of the crippling feeling of belonging to a social group doomed to die out. At this point we should not call too quickly for bold faith, inspired from above and holding out in holy defiance against all secular probabilities. If this were all the advice that could be given, how could the First Vatican Council have spoken of the Church's greatness and fruitfulness in history as a motive of credibility?

The true point and importance of the principle which emerges from the present and future of the little flock, of an offensive attitude towards 'neopaganism' as distinct from one that is merely defensive, can be appreciated only when we coolly recognize that the missionary forces of the Church are in every way finite and very limited. It we don't allow for this fact, the assertion of the principle of missionary strategy will only meet with the unctuous response: Yes, of course, we must do this and not omit that. But if we allow for the limitation of missionary forces and if we really want to achieve even a modest conquest by our offensive, the principle means that we must obviously give up, not all, but certainly a great deal of our defensive strategy. If we understand the principles from this aspect, it will need a lot of courage and find great opposition where it is really to be applied. What this may perhaps mean in the individual case must be considered later.

Here, however, is an example. If in the immediate future we want to choose a capable parish priest or bishop from a number of men, we ought not to ask so much whether the candidate has adapted himself very smoothly to the traditional machinery of the Church or whether he has done well what people expected of him in the light of the traditional behaviour-patterns of office-holders in the Church; we ought to ask rather if he has ever succeeded in getting a hearing from the 'neopagans' and made at least one or two of these into Christians, but not merely by bringing them back to old familiar ways—which is often the result of merely psychological influences. The best missionary in a non-Catholic diaspora situation would be the best candidate for an office in the Church, even though he has hitherto acted perhaps very unconventionally and—for some merely traditional Christians—'scandalously'.

In any case, if the German Church has to be and wants to be understood as a little flock, this is correct in itself but liable to be misunderstood and it has very important and really surprising consequences.

3

CHURCH OF NON-SIMULTANEITY

The German Church is furthermore a Church of unavoidable non-simultaneities, which must be hopefully and lovingly endured. The meaning of this statement should be clear from what we have just said. Secular society consists of historically, culturally, and socially diverse groups which exist at the same moment of time but are not historically and culturally simultaneous; hence the style of Christianity appropriate to each group is different. People formerly were not so explicitly aware of the lack of historical and cultural simultaneity on the part of diverse social groups in the Church, because the majority of church-going Christians belonged to the same rural and lower and middle class urban milieu and their representatives also in secular and ecclesiastical public life maintained a very lively contact with the same milieu, in which they mostly had their roots.

Now, however, not only has this milieu, once the recruitment field of ordinary Christians, become much more pluralistic and differentiated, not only has the specifically modern mentality with its rationalism and social mobility permeated and made its mark on these traditional recruitment areas of church-going Christianity, but the field itself has become far too small if the Church is not to become more and more the little flock in a *wrong* sense: an historically and socially insignificant sect, which life at large passes by unheeding. So the present-day Church is—and the Church of the future will be still more—made up of historically, culturally, and socially non-simultaneous groups. This state of affairs may well be eliminated in the not too distant future through the emergence of a social milieu everywhere and in every respect imprinted with the mentality now prevalent and soon to be predominant.

Apart however from the fact that new and diversified groups unforeseeable today will then again appear in this future society, the German Church *today* is anyway a Church of such non-

simultaneous groups. These groups cannot simply be identified
with the diverse educational layers, although the level of education is certainly a factor in their diversity. But it may well be
and it is relatively easy to see—for example—that a person
very well educated in a formal sense nevertheless lives socially
and according to his true and original, but never sufficiently
explicit mentality in the spirit and feeling of a former epoch
and tries to defend and justify this way of life with all the
resources of his education. This sort of thing is not simply *a
priori* without justification, but it does not take away the force
of the observation that at the same moment of time there are
groups in the same Church which are not at all simultaneous
in spirit.

This situation is also very complex and difficult since we
cannot *a priori* and without more ado assume that something
is obsolete merely because it is defended and regarded as still
valid today and in the future by a 'former' group, culturally
and intellectually belonging to the past. In this sense values
and norms of life which are permanently valid may sometimes
be defended in a really old fashioned way and do not seem
obvious enough to be examined in the light of a more recent
'fashion' and so do not lead to the formation of a new group.
If it is impossible for historical changes of ways of thought,
of feeling for life, of ideals, in brief, of 'consciousness', on the
part of all secular and religious groups, to be synchronized
perfectly, if these non-simultaneous groups inevitably co-exist
simultaneously in the Church, then all that the Christian can
do is to come to terms with the situation, bear it patiently, and
maintain in the Church a unity which is effective in practice in
spite of all the difficulties involved.

In the light of all this, what may be called compromises
simply cannot be avoided: they merely reflect the facts and
try to do justice as far as possible to all these non-simultaneous
groups. Since all the groups in principle certainly have a right
to exist, the fact must be accepted in teaching and in practice
that in the one Church with her one Spirit there can and must
be a variety of charisms whose ultimate harmony perhaps
simply cannot be fully experienced by us in the still continuing
course of history but is perceptible only to the one Lord of
the Church and history; and he is not identical either with

any sort of individual group or with the Church's office-holders.

The legitimacy of such compromises to maintain the Church's unity in the diversity of historically non-simultaneous groups cannot, of course, mean a sham peace and does not remove the necessity of a fair fight among the groups. For the 'younger' group represents the inevitable and necessary continuation of the Church's history in constantly facing new historical situations; the 'older' group may have a mission of planting into the Church's future the inalienable values of the past which, when examined more deeply, can certainly be seen as 'modern' tomorrow. Such compromises can be equally unpleasant for all groups and demand sacrifices. A person who is simply not prepared in the concrete case to make these compromises shows his lack of faith in the permanence of the Church in all the transformations—which he regards as too rapid or too slow— or he over-estimates a factor which cannot be given its full value in such a compromise.

Once again, this ultimate readiness to accept compromises must not be allowed to lead merely to a graveyard peace in the Church or to a situation in which no universally binding decisions are made at all and each is left to do as he likes. A readiness for compromises in real decisions, which are then in principle universally binding (although they should not regulate every detail or impose uniformity in every respect), may lead to compromises only if there has been an honest and realistic struggle, if one group has tried to convince and to be convinced by the other, and if finally there has been a mutually agreed attempt to bring about changes of attitude on the part of non-simultaneous groups.

It is also obvious that such norms and prescriptions for the historically non-simultaneous groups to live together in the Church cannot simply remove the stubbornness and severity of the inevitable struggle among the groups. But this harshness and bitterness can be kept within tolerable limits if each group is self-critical and tries to understand the other group, if people are not too quick to deny the good will or genuine Christianity of both sides.

4

CHURCH OF POLARIZATON AND
GROUP-FORMATION

In the German Church today then there is a great danger of
inhuman and unchristian polarization. The word 'polarization'
is not very clear. But what we are talking about here should be
intelligible. Polarization does not occur merely because there
are differences of opinion (in theology, in the Church's practice,
in regard to the concrete links between the Christian and the
Church on one hand, and secular environment and society on
the other, etc.), but because those who hold such opinions form
themselves into groups in such a way that they no longer truly
live together, pray together, and work together *with* each other:
the individual has to face the dilemma either of belonging
to a particular group or of being regarded as its enemy, or at
least suspected in principle of being hostile; he is forced in each
and every question to ally himself with a particular group; only
those supporters are promoted who have devoted themselves
heart and soul to this particular group; when something new
is proposed, the first question is always whether it suits the group
or is likely to damage its prestige. We are certainly in danger
of this sort of polarization today.

There have always been schools, tendencies, and—if you
like—parties, and so on, in the Church. This is inevitable and
we need not take it too tragically. But the danger of a stupid
and ultimately unfruitful polarization arises from other causes.
People are thoughtless and suspicious of each other; they label
each other 'reactionary' or 'progressive'; they attack each other,
not with relevant arguments, but with outbursts of feeling. Each
group, each periodical, each newspaper, is simply given wholesale approval or wholesale condemnation. Someone who holds
a different opinion is at once assumed by the other to be stupid
or wicked, to be reactionary or a modernist out to destroy
Christianity. There are those who move only in circles which
they feel instinctively to be sympathetic, without first examin-

ing them in a critical spirit. What is new is always accepted
promptly by some as the last word of supreme wisdom and
rejected by others as the greatest danger to Christianity of all
time. This is what is happening among us today.

To some all former positions in theology and in the Church's
life are gradually coming to seem *a priori* old-fashioned, suspect,
debris from the past. To others all that is new, to which they
are not accustomed, which demands painful relinquishing of the
old which has grown dear to them, is already decay and dis-
solution. On the one side the traditional is considered ridiculous
from the standpoint of reason; on the other, revelations and
heavenly apparitions are at hand to show how destructive and
diabolical are those who speak of new ideas, indulge in novel
practices, or want to make these acceptable. And there are
already sufficient people in the German Church for whom even
the Pope is not papal enough and who even question his
authority because they suspect him of heresy.

All reasonable people belonging to these groups in the Church,
which are unavoidable in practice, should resist the unchristian
offensiveness of such polarizations. Of course these naïve and
stupid polarizing tendencies must be resisted not only among
the 'others', but also among those who are closer to us in their
sense of life and on the whole belong to the same group. Individual 'camps' should fight passionately against each polarizations whenever they occur among their own members. Each
of us ought to ask himself whether he has been bold enough
even in criticizing his own friends and whether he has been
so also in public. A Christian ought really to treat his enemies
with more consideration than his friends, but with us sinful
Christians is is mostly the other way round.

We constantly forget that we ourselves and therefore also
our friends are exposed in our shortsightedness, with our narrow
minds and intolerance, uncritically to the mentality of a particular time: whether of today or yesterday is really irrelevant. As
Christians, we are aware that we are sinful men, always con-
ceited, proud, self-assured. We must first and last remind ourselves and our friends of this fact and not only hold it against
those with whom we don't agree. It may of course be said that
all this is obvious, but useless in practice. But what would
remain of Christianity if we were to regard a call for this self-

critical, 'self-denial' *a priori* as empty talk and offensive moral-izing. It is only when we have constantly, conscientiously and self-critically, reminded ourselves that we, too, are and remain self-righteous and narrow-minded people in such controversies within the Church and simply cannot exclude these shocking ingredients completely from our actions, that we may stand up as Christians for our opinion without this being at once de-preciated as polarization; only then should we stand up boldly and militantly for our opinion, even though we know that the future never shows one 'party' to be wholly and solely in the right, but that only the never adequately planned future and therein God are in the right.

If each of us has such a modest idea of himself and his group, then the struggle becomes not only legitimate but definitely permitted and commanded; but—at least to a certain extent—it is liberated from a self-righteous and humourless fanaticism which Christians cannot permit themselves. There remain then diversities of opinion in all dimensions of Christian life and thought, but the necessary unity of faith, of spirit and of love, can remain firm; there is none of that obstinate polarization which is inhuman and unchristian, which forgets that we not only should, but indeed *can* love even our 'enemies', and as long in fact as they remain 'enemies'.

What we have just said still needs some clarification. Groups in the Church, distinguished from each other partly because of their historical non-simultaneity, partly for objective reasons, partly because of diversities of opinion in matters of discretion, may 'organize' themselves even in the most diverse ways as long as these are acceptable to Christianity and the Church. Basis groups, groups of priests, and similar combinations, can-not as such be accused *a priori* of being unchristian or un-catholic. Nor do such groups need *a priori* to emerge with the encouragement or approval of authority, of a bishop or of Rome. They can also be formed spontaneously from below, without being for that reason uncatholic.

When they are formed and they propagate and defend their opinions, they exercise, of course, through their existence and life a certain pressure on the authorities, which the latter do not necessarily feel to be desirable or pleasant. The authorities should not consider such 'pressure' in principle and always unfair; they should not label these groups *a priori* as pressure groups. Whether the 'pressure' is really juridically, humanly, and in Christian terms illegitimate, depends on the precise way in which it is exerted. Pressure is not as such illegitimate merely because certain authorities don't like it or decide that its aims are objectively wrong. This is merely a critical judgement and there is nothing laid down to the effect that authority always judges rightly in all cases.

The working out of an exact casuistry to decide how far pressure is legitimate and when it is illegitimate in a concrete case, simply cannot be avoided. This casuistry would have to make very precise distinctions both with regard to the objectives of such pressure and to the ways in which it attempts to be effective. But in any case the authorities cannot act as if all pressure offering an unwelcome resistance to their own views and tendencies were unchristian and uncatholic; and in any case the groups and their leaders may not act as if any means to the ends which they consider right is for that reason legitimate. Here too the end does not justify every means.

Circumstances may arise in which the Church's social structure and unity can be maintained and in the concrete respected by a particular group only if the group—at least for the time being—refrains from realizing a goal which is legitimate in itself. But woe to the pastors who exploit the respect due to their formal authority to prevent the achievement of a task that is now required for the Church. In an extreme case certainly a group striving for a legitimate goal might have to leave the implementation of such a 'woe' to God and the Church's future history. Anyone who disputes or wants to modify the formal authority of office in the Church, merely because it makes an objectively false decision in a particular case, is undermining ecclesiastical office in principle and tacitly making himself sovereign lord of history. On the other hand, there can be subjectively and objectively cases in which there is a limit to the obedience required in the Church. But this is another question and need not be discussed at length here.

Such groups, possible and legitimate in the Church, need not however lead to the sort of polarizations and confrontations which we have rejected as unchristian and uncatholic. They can struggle seriously and honestly with one another and need not simulate an innocuous peace which does not exist in reality. But they must not and may not regard each other simply as enemies, intent on mutual destruction. They must do everything to live with one another in the midst of the conflict. Each group ought to be struggling also for a better understanding of the other group. For example, why should not one group invite representatives of another group to its meetings and let them speak there? Why can one group not regard the other as a critical authority for itself, of which it has an absolute need?

PART TWO

What are we to do?

We come to the second part of our reflections, to the question: What are we to do? Something has been said about this incidentally in the first part. We must begin here with some primary methodological considerations.

1

PRELIMINARY METHODOLOGICAL CONSIDERATIONS

First of all we must recognize soberly that no planning of the Church's future in the next decades can relieve us of the necessity of going forward into a future that cannot be planned, of risk, of danger, and of hope in the incalculable grace of God. In spite of all futurology, the secular future cannot be known precisely in advance. For, apart from everything else, we cannot know what exactly will be the effects on the mentality of the coming generation of the elements of that future as they are successively attained. If this incalculable secular future is to be the Church's field of action and also helps to determine the Church's activity, it is quite obvious that the Church's future cannot be precisely foreseen and actively planned, even for the next decades.

Even now we are going towards a future of the Church that is still hidden from us. This is the human lot, even of the Church, and something which a Christian attitude of true hope and confidence must really take for granted. If we want, we can console ourselves at the same time with the thought that all futurologists, social scientists, and politicians also know really no more about the future, in spite of all calculations and forecasts; all secular prophecies are constantly being disavowed in whole or in part; things never turn out exactly as well or as badly as had been hoped or feared; neither a promised land nor a final catastrophe will soon take away from us the burden and the dignity of a continuing pilgrimage through history. Nor can a rational and sober futurology of the Church be seriously supplemented by recourse to one or other of the prophecies bandied about in pious circles, since these are merely the expression of an apocalyptic and not an eschatological mentality which cannot at present be extirpated in certain sociological groups. If then in what follows certain forecasts and imperatives for the more immediate future of the Church in

Germany are expounded, it is only with the reservations above-mentioned.

If therefore these perspectives of the future seem vague and commonplace, perhaps mere truisms, it may be asked whether it is possible to say anything better or clearer on these questions and particularly whether the conclusions which might be drawn even from what has been said are in fact being drawn boldly and unambiguously in the German Church. As long as this is not done, as long as merely lip-service is paid for the most part to these consequences, in order to leave everything as it was before and to postpone till tomorrow what could be done for the future today, we must continue to repeat the obvious. At the same time, we must in particular not overlook the fact that the more immediate socio-political future of our people is very uncertain, since very substantial changes—for good or bad—are likely and must be taken into account as far as possible in any programming of the Church's future. But it looks as if this is scarcely considered in the Church's life and planning and as if we were starting out more or less tacitly with the assumption that secular society in the West will remain for the next decades almost as it is now. In this respect of course there is much that cannot be foreseen and therefore many preparations, desirable in themselves, for or against what is coming, are not possible. The gospel warning against taking too much thought for the morrow therefore holds also at the present time. But for what can be foreseen we should still prepare at the opportune time and not simply go on as before and wait like a mouse, hypnotized by the serpent of the future and doing nothing to save itself. Even if we equip ourselves for what can be foreseen of the future, enough remains that is incalculable and can only be awaited in hope and patience.

We know that there is much in the life of the Church which must be covered by imperatives and directives, particularly in so far as it is the object of synodal declarations: this is a factor that must be brought into our reflections on method. This means that it would be wrong and disastrous for the life of the Church, indeed it would render the Church immobile, if we were to regard the Church's decisions as rigorous deductions from the principles of faith and Christian morality, as long as the situation to which the principles are applied is sufficiently clearly understood. There may be cases—even important ones—where this sort of thing is possible. But the Church must reach decisions in very many, often important cases, which cannot simply be deduced conclusively from the binding principles of Christian dogma and morality, even when there is adequate knowledge of the situation; these decisions must be made in the light of our best knowledge and conscience, but also in a creative freedom, and cannot be justified adequately by the merely rational manipulation of Christian principles.

Since we are tempted without reflection, to expect the Church's decisions either to be rationally stringent in the above-mentioned sense or not to be binding at all, the Church becomes as helpless, immobile and inefficient as we so often feel today. We shall have to speak of this again later. But it must be emphasized already in this context, since it is of fundamental importance on planning the future. The future of the Church in Germany cannot be planned and built up merely by the application of generally recognized Christian principles; it needs the courage of an ultimately charismatically inspired, creative imagination.

At the same time, decisions must be made which involve a choice between several conceivable and in themselves defensible possibilities. Decisions must be made, even though they must seem harsh and one-sided, since they are the result of the choice of one out of several possibilities which cannot contain within itself the good that is in all the rest. Compromises can be appropriate and necessary; but if the attempt is made to bring together all that is good in the various possibilities, the compromises will be merely verbal and hollow: all the hares will be chased and none really caught.

In the Church's action with reference to the future and in synodal decisions in which choice is very difficult, the right emphasis must be found. Even the Church cannot equally at all times do everything that comes within the scope of her mission and function. To attempt to do otherwise would mean a failure to do justice to any task and to squander very limited resources in the attempt to deal with everyone and everything simultaneously. At a synod we may discuss where the emphasis has to be placed, at which points it is preferable to apply the finite resources of men, of spiritual energy and material aids. But if we never succeed in finding the right emphasis, if we decide

to do justice to everyone and everything, to attack simultaneously at all points on the Church's front, if we draft an ideal
programme for each and every task of the Church, then we
are certainly wrong. The only certain criterion for avoiding
this capital error seems to me to lie in the fact that not a few
in the Church are protesting, complaining about the choice of
emphasis, and declaring that the Church or the synod has not
taken seriously enough the interests and needs which they represented.

The principle just developed involves also a demand for
courage in certain circumstances to give up tasks and positions
which the Church has hitherto insisted on claiming for herself.
History shows that the Church has often defended positions
against the powers which tried to drive her out of them, attempting to hold them with the utmost force and to the detriment of her ultimate and unavoidable task. It was only when
compelled by violence to abandon them that she noticed and
admitted that they did not have to be defended at all costs and
that her inopportune defence had only injured herself and her
proper task. We might recall, for example, the renunciation of
the papal states: this came far too late, but if it had been
sincerely undertaken at an earlier stage, much would have
turned out for the better in Italy and in the Church.

As a result of a pious shortsightedness in the Church, very
often accompanied by holy zeal and anger against anti-catholic
and anticlerical injustice, positions may well be vacated also
only in the future, although their abandonment would be opportune now and providence would really have nothing against
it. But we should not be too hard on this pious myopia. It may
be unavoidable if it is quite impossible to see a way of recon-
ciling really indispensable tasks involving the Church's claims
with the further historical development of society, if a legitimate
opportunity for the Church to abandon certain positions becomes visible only when this is and has been for a long time
forced upon her. But there are certainly also occasions when
we can prudently foresee and react in advance to an inescapable development requiring the abandonment of certain positions in the Church, without squandering time and resources on
their defence or estranging still more from the Church those
who are bringing about such an historical development.

It seems to me also that the courage to abandon positions no longer tenable means asking modestly, but realistically and insistently, whether it is always possible to take with us on this march in to the Church's future all the fine fellows whose out of date mentality is opposed to a march into the unknown future. For, if we enter on it, we shall be able to keep in the Church or in friendly relations with it not a few who are in any case on the way to the future; but we shall also estrange, shock, and scandalize not a few who feel at home only in the Church as they have been accustomed to see it in the past. Certainly we must modestly and charitably show consideration to these 'conservatives' as far as this is at all possible, but there is no Christian principle to the effect that the conservatives must always be in the right when a choice has to be made between the two groups.

An example, which can scarcely be disputed, may make this clear. If we have only very limited resources for the foreign missions, it is certainly permissible to assign the greater part to the mission to *those* people who represent the greater historical potential for the future of the world and to leave other people simply to God's grace, which is anyway mightier than the Church : thus, for example, it is better to send missionaries to Japan than to the Eskimos. Likewise we may well be right to try more to keep or win for the first time those who are intimately involved in the oncoming future than to keep those who are bringing up the rear of the Church's advance towards a future that will come without fail. It is really true, for example, and not merely an invention of the 'conservatives' that a modern theology and preaching renders some worthy Christians insecure in their traditional faith and leads them into the temptation to give up believing altogether, since they are no longer able to discover their old faith in this modern theology and preaching—although it certainly has an objective existence there. Of course we must do our best to avert this threat to those who believe in the traditional way and to try as far as possible to take them with us into the future of the old faith. But if and in so far as this sort of thing is not possible in the concrete and in practice, it is certainly right to give more consideration to those who believe or are willing to believe and can really achieve their faith in the form in which it exists today or tomorrow than to the stragglers obviously present for historical and sociological reasons.

To win one new man of tomorrow for the faith is more important for the Church than to keep in the faith two men of yesterday; the latter will be saved by God's grace even if the present and future way of proclaiming the faith makes them insecure. God's strategy of salvation and that of the Church are not simply identical. For God's grace is infinite, but the Church's resources are very finite. For the sake of an offensive strategy on the part of the Church, advancing towards the future, we can have the courage in principle—without directly intending it—to be ready to lose today *that* person who would no longer belong to the Church tomorrow: for tomorrow anyway his mentality and social situation will no longer sustain his traditionally constituted faith.

It seems to me that the institutional Church in our country has not considered sufficiently the principle just developed. I would not like to accuse it of positively rejecting or persecuting the Christians of tomorrow, who already exist. Such an accusation would be unjust and evidence merely of hypersensitivity which should be nourished least of all by those who think they belong to the vanguard in an historical development of the life and consciousness of the Church. But it does seem to me that our institutional Church plays the conservatives' game too often in concrete questions, for the most part resisting decisions in favour of the future until they are extorted from it, running groaning behind developments instead of leading these itself with supreme courage.

One thing more must be said about the methodology of planning the future of the Church. It is of those things which are taken for granted, one of the truisms which we constantly overlook in the course of life. Plans for the future must be made at the opportune time. If for instance we know that in ten years time we shall be able to provide only half of the existing parishes with a priest on the spot, we must take incisive measures today in order to meet the state of affairs which will soon be with us. Such timely planning is necessary if only because opportunities and their preconditions are now present for what will be required later. If we go on as we have been doing these will disappear, since they will not have been tested in practice and subjected to experiments. If today, for instance, men who have proved themselves in their life, calling, and marriage, were perhaps ready to be ordained and to take on the leadership of a parish, their example could be beneficial for a time which is approaching when they will be absolutely necessary and when such a vocation will be completely taken for granted; but if it is attempted only after another ten or twenty years, there will be nobody who is prepared to take on the task. Opportune planning and opportune execution of the plan must take place at a time when the project is not yet absolutely pressing or obvious to everybody. But, for that very reason, there will be internal and external opposition to such projects, which will only too easily provide an excuse for postponing them to later times. But in reality planning and execution are timely only if they come before a judgement can be expected on the part of the average person. By then the time is more than ripe, but we don't notice it.

To these somewhat unmethodological methodological considerations must be added the readiness to leave the Spirit to rule the Church as he wills, whenever we can see with any degree of clarity that he is at work. No one in the Church will reject this policy in principle, but very often we demand criteria for the breathing of God's Spirit in the Church which in their practical application are incapable of revealing the presence of the Spirit at all. The Spirit breathes too in earthly human beings. But for that very reason his breathing is mingled always with human motivations, one-sidedness and precipitance. If people exploit such human weakness as proof that it has nothing at all to do with the activity of the Spirit, they will not be able to discover him anywhere and will find it easy to show that only human beings are at work and not the Spirit of God.

2

ROMAN CATHOLIC CHURCH

We are and we shall remain also in the future the *Roman* Catholic Church. This in itself is obvious, but it needs to be stated clearly today, in view of a widespread theoretical and practical allergy to Rome. To stress this does not mean that we are supporters of the movement for 'Pope and Church', but only that the relationship of Christianity and the Church to Rome is absolutely necessary for us Catholics and not merely the result of historical or sociological accidents.

Criticism and a critical attitude in principle towards the Church belong to the essence of Christianity and of the Catholic faith itself. The Pope's concrete function in the Church is also an historical factor and its history is still obviously always open towards the future. Often enough individual popes in the past 150 years have provided and still provide today an occasion for criticism even of the institution itself and of what is claimed to be normal practice. The Petrine ministry, for us a matter of faith, may be conceived and required by the situation of the modern world in a very different concrete shape. But all this by no means implies that we have a right to contradict in theory or practice the conception of the Petrine ministry taught by the First and Second Vatican Council.

Paul's opposition to Peter, described in the Epistle to the Galatians, certainly has still a meaning for us today. The style of papal devotion as it developed particularly in the nineteenth century may rightly seem to many to belong to a vanished age. The tiara has been abolished and now particularly we have the right, even for binding dogmatic reasons, to reject the claim of the *Civiltà cattolica* that our own faith and our own religious life flow from the Pope. We assign to the papacy a quite definite function in the Church, which is nothing like that of the head of a totalitarian state. This function is sustained and embraced by the greater spirit and life of the Church; it is sustained in its binding force for ourselves by our primal faith in Jesus

Christ and his Church which is greater than the papacy. The Pope's universal function in regard to the whole Church can be described only to a limited degree and analogously in terms of juridical categories borrowed from a secular society and which hold even there only in a way that is very much historically conditioned.

A great deal which is possible but not dogmatically stringent, which is historically conditioned and changeable, and which as such still holds today in the papacy's concrete function, permits us to hope rightly for a further change. Such hopes can be very emphatically asserted, even though they do not authorize any revolution in the Church, not even in regard to this fundamentally changeable factor, and must not lead to a disruption of the historical continuity and function of the papacy: thus they must always take the form of a hope (ultimately eschatologically substantiated) that changes will come about through the papacy itself and not against it. None of this alters the dogmatic fact that the papacy belongs to the binding content of our faith itself, in its proper place within the hierarchy of truths and in our own Christian life. This holds absolutely.

However justified we may be in our critical reservations in regard to the concrete form of the papacy, these should not prevent us from approaching it even in this concreteness with *that* unemotional, realistic understanding with which the concrete form of Christianity itself in all its dimensions and areas has to be lovingly and impartially accepted at any particular time, although we know that this concrete shape is not simply identical with the essence of Christianity but is historically changeable. An irritable and embittered allergy to this concrete shape of the papacy is profoundly uncatholic. Today we can boldly but also patiently and effectively face the concrete shape of the papacy in a critical spirit without succumbing to this sort of irritable allergy towards it.

Just as in secular society there is or must be not only social criticism, but also a genuine and impartial, deliberate acceptance of the state, so there should be an analogous approach to the papacy. Its critics should not only or primarily be on the look out for real or supposed encroachments of this supreme ministry in the Church and trying to ward them off, but ought to reflect constructively on how this Petrine ministry presumably could and should undertake *new* tasks of a *positive* character in a number of directions in a Church which is preparing today to be really a World-Church and is facing a unified world with tasks which can be fulfilled only by a worldwide Church that is *institutionally* one. If the worldwide movement of Marxist socialism proclaims a 'democratic centralism' to be the structure of the social order, we can always take into account the fact that this concept can be and is interpreted in a variety of ways. We can insist that the Church is not a secular reality, but has quite a different nature. But the Church cannot be a debating society: it must be able to make decisions binding on all within it. Such a demand cannot be *a priori* contrary to man's dignity, if—as people today are never tired of impressing upon us—he is indeed a social being. And then a supreme point at which all reflections and democratic discussions are turned into universally binding decisions cannot be without meaning.

It might certainly be desirable for decision-making processes in the Church to take place with the active co-operation of as many people as possible and to be clearly visible to all. We must certainly insist that they are in accordance with the facts and that even the preference of a majority as such is itself one of the facts to be taken into account. But we should not act as if all such decision-making processes, after sufficient reflection, could be broken down into rationally demonstrable processes, understood by all; as if individual and personal factors, which cannot be completely analysed, played no part at all in them; as if a community decision were not in fact the decision of a few of its representatives. Hence a 'monarchical' head (in a sense which certainly requires precise definition) is certainly appropriate even in the Church and is really inevitable: it does not need to be defended by paternalistic ideologies. This inevitability is better protected against dangers when it is not concealed, not suppressed, but when safeguards for its appropriate and visible exercise are built into its permanent function (*jure humano* and in a way that corresponds to the diversity of the social situation and to special fields for which decisions have to be made).

In this respect there is certainly much that must be improved and renewed in the *concrete* structure of the supreme office in the Church if it is really to be efficient and visible to the extent necessary today. But it is precisely today that we should see positively the necessity of an efficient supreme headship of the Church and not think that the more it is restricted in practice, the more we are corresponding to the demands of the time. We should also appreciate the fact that *no* juridical structure can *a priori* exclude mistaken decisions and abuses. We should appreciate the fact that we simply cannot as Christians and Catholics have an impartial attitude to such an office unless it implies also a hope—which cannot be secured by laws and institutions—in the Spirit in the Church.

3

A DECLERICALIZED CHURCH

The Church should be a declericalized Church. This proposition is of course open to misunderstanding and must be explained. It is obvious that there are offices in the Church with definite functions and powers, however these offices may be distinguished and divided, however the functions and powers transmitted to office-holders in the concrete can or must be precisely conceived. It is also obvious, in the light of the Church's nature, mission, and spirit, that her offices and office-holders as such have a special character that is not shared by offices and office-holders in secular society. But this special feature comes to these offices and these office-holders as such precisely from the nature of the Church as Spirit-filled community of all who believe in Jesus Christ. It does not originate in a way which would simply dissociate offices and office-holders from the Church as the community of all Christians.

Office has a functional character in the Church as society, even though this society with its functions (proclamation of the word, sacrament, leadership of the Church's life as society) constitutes a sign of what is real in the Church: the free Spirit, faith, hope, love, to which all socially institutional factors in office are orientated and at the same time are never identical with them. Hence the 'hierarchy' (if we may use the term) in the real nature of the Church is not identical with the hierarchy in the Church's social structure. The situation in the Church is really like that of a chess club. Those who really support the club and give it its meaning are the members, to the extent that they play chess well. The hierarchy of the club leadership is necessary and appropriate if and as far as it serves the community of chess players and their 'hierarchy' and does not think it is identical with the latter or that it can play chess better simply in virtue of its function.

So too office is to be respected in the Church; but those who love, who are unselfish, who have a prophetic gift in the Church, constitute the real Church and are far from being always identical with the office-holders. It is of course part of the Catholic faith that the Spirit of God in the Church is able to prevent an absolute schism between those who simply possess the Spirit and those who hold office and therefore the latter also in virtue of their social function—but only in the last resort—enjoy a certain gift of the Spirit. As soon as these obvious dogmatic truths are lived and practised impartially and taken for granted by office-holders and other Christians, then we have what we call a declericalized Church: that is, a Church in which the office-holders too in joyous humility allow for the fact that the Spirit breathes where he will and that he has not arranged an exclusive and permanent tenancy with them. They recognize that the charismatic element, which can never be completely regulated, is just as necessary as office to the Church: that office is never simply identical with the Spirit and can never replace him; that office too is really effectively credible in the sight of men only when the presence of the Spirit is evident and not merely when formal mission and authority are invoked, however legitimate these may be.

If we also remember (and this must be specially considered at greater length later) that the Church of the future must grow in its reality quite differently from the past, from below, from groups of those who have come to believe as a result of their own free, personal decision, then what is meant here by declericalization may become clearer. Office will exist in a Church growing from below in this way, really and not merely theoretically emerging from the free decision of faith on the part of individuals, since there cannot be a society at all without office. It can then rightly be said that this office rests on the mission from Christ and not merely on the social combination of individual believers, even though it is also true that this mission from above is included in God's gracious will to all men, to which the Church owes her nature and existence. But this official authority will be really effective in future in virtue of the obedience of faith which believers give to Jesus Christ and his message. It will no longer be effective in virtue of powers over society belonging to office in advance of this obedience of faith, as it is today but to a constantly diminishing extent.

In this sense the authority of office will be an authority of freedom. In practice, in future, the office-holders will have as much effective authority—not merely a theoretical claim to authority—as is conceded to them freely by believers through their faith. The assumption of an authority in the Church will always have to consist in an appeal to the free act of faith of each individual and must be authorized in the light of this act in order to be effective at all; in the concrete the office-holder's appeal to his authority will be a proclamation of *faith*. For it is only through this faith that authority becomes really effective; the Church is a declericalized Church in which the believers gladly concede to the office-holders in free obedience the special functions in a society—and thus also in the Church—which cannot be exercised by all at the same time.

It is true that these official powers in the Church are conferred by a special rite which we call the sacrament of Holy Order and, when they are conferred, the office-holders are also assured by God of the help of that Spirit who is with the Church; but this in no way alters the declericalized conception of office in the Church. In the future questions or doubts about office will no longer be effectively dismissed by appealing to the formal authority of office, but only by furnishing proof of a genuinely Christian spirit on the part of the office-holder himself. He will gain recognition for his office by being genuinely human and a Spirit-filled Christian, one whom the Spirit has freed for unselfish service in the exercise of his social function in the Church.

We might ask now what conclusions are to be drawn from this declericalization for the office-holders' way of life in the concrete. The life-style especially of the higher clergy even today sometimes conforms too much to that of the 'managers' in secular society. All the ceremony which distinguishes the office-holder even in the most ordinary circumstances from the mass of the people and other Christians and which has nothing to do with the exercise of his office and stresses his dignity where it is out of place, might well disappear. In the very exercise of office there could certainly be much greater objectivity in judging and deciding and, particularly for outsiders, the attempt to be objective could be made more clearly visible. There is no point in being secretive. An appeal to 'experience' becomes suspect when experience appears to have been condi-

tioned from the beginning by clerical prejudices. If advisers
have been consulted, we ought to be allowed to know who they
were. Office loses none of its authority or dignity if the decision
and the reasons for it are made public at the same time. The
more secular from the nature of the case is the object of a
decision, so much the more relevant are *those* reasons which
can be understood even by someone who is not well versed in
theology.

There must be more courage to reverse and withdraw decisions
without a false and ultimately unchristian concern for prestige
and also to admit it openly if these decisions have turned out
to be objectively mistaken or—humanly speaking—unjust.
Reaction to criticism of decisions must be relaxed and open to
enlightenment, not every time taking the form of asserting that
the matter has been considered so thoroughly that the decision
made is beyond all criticism. In matters also which are dogmatically and constitutionally by no means immutable, we
should remember that the simple wish of a majority in the
Church quite legitimately counts even in advance as part of the
objective substantiation of a decision. A decision to be based
merely on the weight of custom must not be decked out with
ideological arguments produced for the occasion by smart
theologians or church-functionaries: these might seem very
profound, but they really convince only those who have already
been convinced for a long time for other reasons of what is now
propped up by subtle theological or legal arguments. The danger
of self-delusion through such subsequent ideological substructures is very great in the Church and it is a typical feature
of false clericalism.

No damage is done to office or office-holders if the latter
honestly admit uncertainties, doubts, the need of experiment
and further reflection, without knowing the outcome, and don't
behave as if they had a direct hot line to heaven to obtain an
answer to each and every question in the Church. The formal
authority of an office, even when the office-holder exercises it
legitimately, does not relieve him of the duty, in the light of
the question before him and within really contemporary horizons
of understanding, of effectively winning a genuine assent on the
part of those affected by his decision. It seems to me that Roman
decrees in particular do not sufficiently take account of this

principle, and therefore in such enactments too much weight is laid on Rome's formal authority. Particularly in moral theological doctrinal decisions, it cannot be claimed on the one hand that they relate to natural law which is in principle intelligible to everyone, while on the other hand invoking the merely formal teaching authority, without any adequate attempt to expound convincingly and vividly in the language of the present time the intrinsic arguments derived from the nature of the case. Many other similar and proximate and remote conclusions could be drawn from a correctly understood declericalization of office in the Church. But this may suffice for the moment.

4

A CHURCH CONCERNED WITH SERVING

The Church in Germany ought to be a Church concerned not with itself, but with men, with all men. This was said at the Second Vatican Council and has been said often enough since then. But this requirement is still far from deciding the attitude of churchgoing Christians and the Church. A social group which is constantly harried and nevertheless will not and cannot give way, is inevitably under a great temptation to think mainly of itself and its continued existence. This is also the situation with us.

If the Church cares about people—and, thank God, it does, to an extent which should by no means be concealed from the non-churchgoing public who certainly do no more—this care is conceived in an odd sort of way and presented as an apology for the Church itself, it becomes too easily a means to the end. But the Church with all its institutions is itself a means for men and they are its end.

Office-holders and clerics particularly are liable to become ecclesiological introverts. They think of the Church, not of people. They want to see the Church free, but not human beings. Under National Socialism, for instance, we thought considerably more about ourselves and about upholding what belonged to the Church and its institutions, than about the fate of the Jews. This may be understandable; but it was not very Christian or very Catholic, if we appreciate the true nature of the Church.

This task of the Church, to exist for men and not for herself, is not merely directed to making men Christians in the sense of churchgoing people. A task understood in this way would really be legitimate only if it were at the same time a matter of winning people who would themselves help to sustain the Church's mission to exist for everybody. If the Church is indeed the sacrament of salvation for a world where in fact most people are saved without the Church's institutionalized means (however much these are willed and authorized by God); if, in spite of her mission, the Church cannot maintain that there is no salvation nor slow healing of the world without her visible manifestation; then to gain new churchgoing Christians means not so much or primarily saving those who would otherwise be lost, but acquiring witnesses as signs making clear for all the grace of God effective throughout the world.

The wish to bring people into the Church, therefore, must be a determination to make these churchgoing Christians serve everyone, even those who are ready to accept their services but nevertheless despise and oppose them; the poor too, the old, the sick, those who have come down in the world, the people on the edge of society, all those who have no power themselves and can bring no increase of power to the Church.

The Church has to stand up for justice and freedom, for man's dignity, even when it is to her own detriment, even when an alliance—perhaps tacit—with the ruling powers would at first sight seem beneficial to her. Certainly none of us would deny this in theory. But, since we are a Church of sinners, we certainly cannot say that we would never in practice betray this essential mission of the Church. We are constantly failing in this respect in the life of the Church and indeed quite certainly even when it comes to official decisions, even in her concrete, institutionalized forms, which of course are themselves marked by the sin of egoism, of the quest for power, of a short-sighted wish for self-assertion. If we are convinced that much injustice and tyranny prevail in a sinful world, if we really are, or might be convinced, that sin also characterizes social structures and is not merely something that happens to private individuals and is characteristic of their deeds, then we ought also really to be surprised how seldom—apart from direct and express attacks on the Church—the Church comes into conflict with those who hold power. This ought to make us suspicious of ourselves; it ought to make us suspicious of some of the conservatism in our midst.

We are not merely uttering pious platitudes, fit only for Sunday sermons, when we say that the Church must not be concerned with serving others merely for the sake of proving her own claims and that she must stand by the side of the poor, the oppressed, life's failures. But does the reality correspond to this sacred principle, the principle that the Church has to be there for all and therefore also for the others, that she must serve even those who attach no importance to her and regard her as a relic from a vanished age? Is this form of the 'folly of the cross' very much in evidence among us? Is enough love applied in the Church, is there enough courage for stubborn confrontations, and are enough power, time, and money given to unselfish service for others, without calculating the advantages to the Church herself? There are of course miracles of love and unselfish service among us and perhaps others are no better on the whole. This, however, does not prove that the Church is wholly the unselfish servant for the welfare and salvation of the others and that we must not always be asking anxiously whether we are not fearfully introverted, concerned more for the Church than for others; it does not relieve individual Christians of the obligation to protest boldly in certain circumstances, even against the office-holders of the Church, when the Church thinks more of herself and tries to save herself otherwise than by saving others. All this is very abstract and its practical meaning really ought to be made clearer by concrete examples. But this is simply not possible here. The brevity of these hints should not lead us to think that the matter is not of the greatest importance.

5

MORALITY WITHOUT MORALIZING

The Church should be one which defends morality boldly and unambiguously, without moralizing. Quite certainly the message of Christianity includes a complex of moral principles. This proposition is correct, independently of the question whether and to what extent moral norms are part of the deposit of revelation or stem from the largely historically conditioned and change-able situation of man and society, receiving a higher motivation and urgency from man's orientation by grace to the immediacy of God in eternal life only in so far as they are relevant at a particular time. A part of the courage to preach this gospel message, in season or out of season, is also the determination resolutely and unambiguously to stand up for this complex of moral principles.

If, however, we put forward this undoubtedly basic and still very relevant principle, we must honestly add that it is not always so easy and clear to say how these concrete questions of human morality are to be answered both in the light of the Christian message and with regard to the present situation. Whether it is congenial or uncongenial, in spite of all com-plaints that we are rendering many people in the Church insecure in their moral conscience, it must be said that there are not a few concrete principles and patterns of behaviour which for-merly—and quite rightly in the circumstances—counted as binding, concrete expressions of the ultimate Christian moral principles, but today are not necessarily binding always and in every case; that perhaps, on the other hand, some moral impera-tives ought now to be defended very concretely, much more clearly and boldly than they are in fact defended, since they were not and could not have been formerly so explicit in the Church's moral consciousness.

Moral consciousness has in fact a history and this history is not merely something added externally to man, while most of the moral principles proclaimed by the Church can be derived from his essential nature; it is rather an intrinsic factor in man's concrete nature, which has a history of its own. Without detriment to man's ultimate, essential consistency, which however can never be filtered off adequately and in chemical purity from the concrete and always historical nature, this concrete human nature has itself a real history and is subject to an internal and social mutation. Such a change, however, can render no longer binding many a feature of the concrete moral norms which were formerly and quite rightly proclaimed as binding, because they corresponded to man's concrete nature at the time; and it can also give an immediate relevance to norms which hitherto had no actual binding force and did not exist in the Church's moral consciousness.

Connected if not identified with this is the fact that Christian morality is to a very considerable extent an 'end morality'. In the individual and social sphere it is certainly possible to play fast and loose with the term by questioning, in the light of this end morality, the binding force of a moral principle which is directly relevant. But, in principle and in the last resort, Christian morality is an end morality, since every Christian is bound in principle by an *absolute* obligation ('under pain of mortal sin') to a *perfect* love of God and neighbour in thought and deed and yet (as distinct from a Protestant view of man's radical sinfulness, involving him in a constant state of guilt) it cannot be said that this absolute obligation binds us at every moment to the most perfect realization then possible in a concrete deed: man is therefore also permitted and simultaneously required to remain open to a further evolution of his own reality and to a higher actualization of his moral consciousness. This holds of the individual in his own particular sphere and of the individual in a society in the process of a moral evolution; it holds likewise of a particular society and of mankind as a whole.

This, of course, is not the place to apply such reflections and principles to particular moral questions. But what has been merely suggested here must be thought out, more deeply studied, and boldly applied to particular questions of Christian morality when the Church sets out to proclaim moral norms today. If she does not do this adequately, the proclamation will sound old-fashioned and unrealistic, the Church will be reproached—and not necessarily or always wrongly—not for proclaiming the moral principles flowing from man's nature and sustained by the basic Christian ethos, but for defending patterns of behaviour which belong to a past epoch of man's history and are not noticed as such by the Church's office-holders, simply because they, too, in their outlook belong to a passing or past age. Examples from recent times which are no longer disputed today even by the most conservative moral theologians can easily be listed.

This is not to dispute the possibility in principle that the Church herself, through deciding for a line of conduct which is itself again an element in man's concrete nature—and therefore binding—can take an active part in shaping the concrete history of moral consciousness, not merely noticing that this history has in fact happened or drawing conclusions from a history which she has not helped to shape. This sort of thing however is not possible through a merely pedantic, ineffective insistence on concrete moral principles, but only through a deed and its appropriate proclamation which really change the historical situation, the concrete nature of man and the total moral consciousness of society.

If we say that the Church must be a moral institution without moralizing, this does not relieve her of the obligation of standing up unambiguously and boldly for the Christian message, even in its moral demands. We are moralizing if we expound norms of behaviour peevishly and pedantically, full of moral indignation at a world without morals, without really tracing them back to that innermost experience of man's nature, which is the source of the so-called principles of natural law and which alone gives them binding force; we are moralizing if moral principles are not traced back to that innermost core of the Christian message which is the message of the living Spirit, the message of freedom from merely external law, the message of love which is no longer subject to any law when it prevails.

This holds particularly today. We have first and last to announce to modern man the innermost blessed, liberating mystery which we call God, redeeming him from fear, from the self-estrangement of his existence. We must show modern man at least the beginning of the way that leads him credibly and concretely into the liberty of God. Where someone has not had an initial experience of God and of his Spirit, liberating him from his deepest fears and from guilt, there is no point in announcing the moral norms of Christianity to him. He would not be able to understand them; at best, they might seem to him to be the source of still more radical constraints and still deeper fears. If a person is not really genuinely and personally in the presence of God (and this cannot be achieved by a little externally indoctrinating talk about God), he may perhaps understand that offences against certain moral norms relating to the concrete nature of the individual and of society are inappropriate; but he cannot understand and realize just what Christianity means by sin and guilt in God's sight.

When we consider this, we may well think that the Church's proclamation contains too much moralizing. Truly Christian morality has man in view, defends him and his open history, arises from the centre of his being: a centre indeed where the Spirit of God is alive, making his demands from within. Christian morality therefore must not create the impression that it is a matter of God's arbitrary legislation, imposing restraints on man, that it is a law coming upon him merely from outside and might well—from man's standpoint—be different. When modern man gets the impression that the Church's morality is a matter of inculcating laws which are not the concrete expression of the impulse of the Spirit liberating man from within, it is evident that we are moralizing and not really proclaiming Christian morality as it must be proclaimed.

Protests against moralizing morality are not merely negative; in the last resort they have positive implications. It is a fact that man and his environment, in so far as they can and should be made subject to his knowledge and control, have become much more complex and unfathomable than formerly. Because they were formerly more simple, at least in so far as they were under man's control at all, because they were also much more stable and unchangeable, it was possible to assert relatively simple and stable norms of behaviour, by which man could come to terms with himself and his environment. The consequences of what a person might do had already been often tested and could be sufficiently clearly foreseen; it was therefore possible to provide very clear moral norms of behaviour, which were relatively simple to manage. This does not alter the fact that these norms were always difficult for man and demanded moral effort for their observation. Today these human realities are both much more complex and at the same time left to man's control to a greater extent; they include elements which formerly simply did not exist as objects on which man could exercise his freedom and thus did not demand any moral norms. This very much more complex world, however, is for that reason much more difficult to understand and therefore no longer so easily provides simple and manageable norms for man and for the Church.

The Church too therefore, in many fields of human life, is often helpless when asked not for quite general and abstract, but for concrete and directly applicable norms. If nevertheless she acts or were to act as if she possessed always and everywhere and for all cases such directly applicable norms, she would simply destroy her credibility by her terrifyingly naïve attitude to life. But if, as a result, the Church is told to stop handing out these prescriptions, costing nothing, by petty clerics living remote from real life, from society, and from modern culture, and to leave such decisions to the conscience of the individual, this demand too may often be crude and over-hasty; the term 'conscience' may be used to cover subjective arbitrariness and whims, which have nothing to do with a self-critical conscience responsible before God and really fearing the possibility of genuine sin. In spite of all this, in principle and rightly understood, such a demand is very often true. Rightly understood, it does not mean the retreat of Christianity and the Church from the field of morals, but a very important change of emphasis in Christian proclamation: consciences must be formed, not primarily by way of a casuistic instruction, going into more and more concrete details, but by being roused and trained for autonomous and responsible decisions in the concrete, complex situations of human life which are no longer completely soluble down to the last detail, in fields never considered by the older morality, precisely because they were then unknown and even now cannot be adequately mastered by a rational casuistry. Where this sort of thing was not possible in the past, probabilism might be brought in to show that a particular course of action was morally indifferent.

Today we see that there are many things which cannot be covered at all by moral theory or casuistry and nevertheless may be matters of conscience of the greatest moment. Here evidently we have a form of moral decision which was not considered at all adequately in traditional moral theology. Unfortunately we cannot discuss this further here. Such a logic of existential decision, on which people formerly reflected only with reference to very secondary decisions of conscience—as, for instance, the choice of a vocation to the priesthood—is an urgent desideratum for a real training of conscience, which today can no longer be accomplished merely by purifying the relevant moral norms. If the effort of moral theology and preaching were to be directed on these lines, there would be less need to moralize and yet in consciences and in the world there would be more genuine morality. The moral decisions even of Christians would then indeed presumably continue to fall materially into many individual questions; but, in spite of their diversity, they would be sustained by a responsibility before God and before man's dignity in justice and love, and there would presumably be more harmony in matters that are really decisive for his enduring substance and his dignity than there is when we moralize and thus cease to be credible, wanting to save morality by an ever more exact and detailed casuistry supposedly universally applicable.

Such a non-moralizing morality however must not suggest that all life's concrete problems would be solved simply by invoking God. They are not solved in this way. Concrete moral problems are frequently intramundane, factual problems, in face of which a Christian is mostly as helpless as other men. Even an appeal to God and his gospel does not produce concrete answers to such concrete problems as the population explosion, hunger in the world, the structure of a future society offering more freedom and justice. When someone has a genuine relationship to God, freed from an ultimate existential dread, he can reflect with a more open mind and freer heart on such problems and look more hopefully for solutions; but this is still a long way from actually finding the solutions which really meet the case.

It is indeed true that today, as in former times, simply appealing to God may involve the danger of reducing religion to the 'opium of the people' (not that this slogan can be regarded as a legitimate argument against religion or faith). God does not relieve us of our secular problems; he does not spare us our helplessness. In the Church therefore we should not act as if he did. In the last resort, even the appeal to God forces us into a radical helplessness. For he is the incomprehensible mystery which forbids us to regard any sort of brightness of our own in our life as the light of eternity. We come to terms with this final helplessness only by surrendering ourselves in hope and love to this incomprehensible God, in a holy 'agnosticism' of capitulation to him who never guaranteed that all our calculations would work out smoothly if only we got on well with him.

6

CHURCH WITH OPEN DOORS

We must be a Church with open doors. This requirement, of course, touches very closely on what has already been said in the third and fourth chapters of this second part. But there is still something more to be added. In former times, even in social and religio-sociological terms, the Church could divide human beings straightforwardly, simply, and clearly, into two classes: those who through baptism and their profession of faith undoubtedly belong to her and those who do not yet belong to her because they are not baptized or no longer belong to her as a result of their public profession of heterodox belief, of their open abandonment of Christianity altogether, or of their excommunication by ecclesiastical authority.

Certainly neither the theological nor the social importance of baptism for membership of the Church should be disputed; but according to Catholic teaching, apart from everything else, the mere fact of being baptized does not in itself constitute full and real membership of the Church. This should be particularly obvious in an age when mere ritual forms are regarded with the most profound distrust. The other factors, however, which constitute full membership of the Church are not as easy to establish now as they were or at least seemed to be in former times. Merely registered membership* of a denominational Church is certainly not equivalent to membership in the genuinely personal and theological sense. A really Christian faith is necessary for this.

Formerly it was supposed to be comparatively easy to decide

---

* In Germany registered membership means not only membership of a church but also commitment to pay the church-tax to the State. Many people are registered simply to ensure the right to church marriage and burial and baptism for their children, but otherwise do nothing about their membership. If a person ceases to be a Christian or changes his religious allegiance, he reports this to the civil authorities in order that he may cease to pay the tax or ensure that his tax goes to his new denomination.

when this Christian faith was present as the basis of church-membership: it was taken as a fact or at least presumed to exist in anyone who was baptized, did not expressly and publicly reject the Christian faith, was living at the same time in a denominationally relatively homogeneous society, and had not officially left the Church. In these conditions it was practically impossible to conceive how such a person could seriously entertain opinions of which he was convinced and which at the same time were opposed to the Christian faith. Today in a pluralistic society it is certainly very different. If a person does not quite explicitly and publicly make a firm profession of the Christian faith—and this is far from being established by registered denominational membership or necessarily assured by some sort of practice of religion—it is not certain that, as a so-called Christian in this pluralistic society, he really possesses *that* faith which is necessary for church-membership in the theological sense. And in practice this faith can by no means be established with the majority of registered denominational Christians; nor do the Churches make any attempt to establish it.

The theologically relevant frontiers of the Churches and the Church are obscure and certainly very fluid. It may, however, be noted in passing that we must not make it too easy to bridge the gap between the official faith of a Church and the actual faith or fragments of faith in the heads and hearts of the majority of registered denominational Christians by appealing to a *fides implicita*. In some cases this may be theologically objectively correct, but in most cases *fides implicita* as explicit faith in the Church's teaching as such, as absolutely normative for the faith of the individual, can by no means be presumed to exist. We have therefore, theologically speaking, a Church whose extent is by no means clearly defined. There are a large number of human beings who belong to the Church in terms of sociology of religion, by virtue of their traditions, familiar habits, childhood influences, and a kind of folklore, but not in a properly theological sense. But if this is the situation in any case and cannot by any means be altered, we should be careful also about the theological qualification we attach to those who do not belong to the church as registered members or because of their birth. In many cases they scarcely differ from many who are within the Church from the standpoint of sociology of religion. The difference between these two groups lies in contingent religio-sociological factors and not in a theological factor. And therefore both groups can be given equal treatment.

So we come finally to what is really meant by 'open doors'. Of course religio-sociological membership of the Church has also a certain theological significance, because and in so far as it is one factor (but only one) in properly theological membership of the Church. To that extent the two groups still remain theologically distinct from one another. But this distinction is of little theological weight compared to the fact that the two groups are occasionally not distinguished in regard to the faith on which membership is based, particularly if we assume that there are baptized people in both. But it then follows that the Church can and should treat both groups more or less equally.

The Church should consider the fluidity and indefiniteness of her frontiers in a *positive* way. She should consider as belonging to her rather than as separated from her those who cannot yet identify themselves with the Church through their faith, but regard her with positive good will as the concrete bearer of the Christian idea. For this is her attitude also towards those who belong to her as registered members, although they are far from possessing certainly the faith which constitutes membership of the Church. Those who are thus close to the Church should not be given the impression that she is interested in them only when they are palpably candidates for self-identification by faith with the institutional Church. If we admit at all—as we must—that even in our historical and social conditions someone may not be a Christian, still less a denominational Christian, and yet be without personal fault, then this holds particularly for those who have a lively interest in the life of the Church, in her task in the world, in intellectually elucidating the Christian faith. They are really in our time what used to be called catechumens: the catechumenate does not begin only when someone firmly declares his decision to become a full member of the Church.

We must oppose the very widespread feeling that a person must be either a committed member of the Church as the result of a personal decision, with all the obligations resulting from this, or necessarily hostile or absolutely indifferent towards the

Church. This feeling, without reflection, is often the reason why older, mature people no longer find their way back to the Church from which they dissociated themselves in earlier years, perhaps in the last resort inculpably. From a theological standpoint, returning to the Church by no means always has to be the homecoming of the prodigal son, the finding of the lost sheep. This sort of return to the Church is only made more difficult when it is conceived *a priori* and always only in the light of such ideal types.

Today particularly there are open doors in the Church, through which individuals, in the history of whose moral and intellectual development there is no really personal mortal sin, may once depart and then return. Although in principle it cannot be his final destiny, all that is possible in practice for an individual may be to settle down mentally and morally in the wider orbit of the Church. If love of neighbour requires us to treat no one as an enemy in the ultimate meaning of the word, then Christians are certainly permitted and morally required to consider these marginal settlers as brothers, without suggesting at every turn that they are not really in the Church and not Christians in the true sense. To adopt the language of Augustine, these people may 'at heart' belong to the Church in a way that is more efficacious for salvation than that of some Christians who belong to the 'body', who are in the Church merely in a religio-sociological sense. None of this, of course, provides any pastoral-theological directives for making the Church one with open doors. But that is not our task here. All that we can do is to indicate the points at which a theological understanding of the situation may be acquired.

In this connection, a word may be said about orthodoxy in the Church. It is obvious that there can be no further talk of the orthodoxy which is essential to the Church, where there is no acknowledgement of the living God of eternal life and of Jesus as mediator of salvation or where these things are shut out by pure humanism or 'horizontalism'. Anyone who does not acknowledge the living God and Jesus as Lord is outside the Church. Even a Church with open doors is not a fair where each and every opinion can set up a stall. It remains true that the Church can have the right and duty to declare authoritatively and unambiguously that this or that doctrine cannot be put forward in the Church as Christian or Catholic. It would be naïve to think that there could never again be anything like an anathema in the future. There is also an hysterical fear of such a clear demarcation of frontiers: a fear that is particularly unjustified today when a false teacher who dissociates himself from the Church is neither *a priori* denied intelligence and good will nor his chance of salvation questioned, if—as we must assume—he defends his opinion as a matter of conscience.

This of course is far from a solution of the problem of orthodoxy in the Church today. The problem is acute today because it is more difficult than ever to decide whether certain theological propositions and opinions lie within the limits of the necessary orthodoxy and unity of the Church or have already overstepped them. It is more difficult to decide this today because a quite considerable theological pluralism simply cannot be avoided and even has a positive function in the Church, since otherwise it would be impossible properly to relate the one gospel to the diversity of horizons of understanding, productive ideas, mentalities, and so on in the world. We must therefore venture only with the utmost caution and modesty to formulate a judgement to the effect that certain theological positions are unorthodox.

Presumably, however, there is something like a straightforward 'discernment of spirits' which will help us to get through on questions of orthodoxy. If a theologian attempts to interpret positively the official teaching of the Church without rejecting this flatly or from top to bottom; if he does not merely express his critical reservations, but stands up positively and seeks lovingly to win people for faith in God and Jesus Christ; if he is not merely a critic, but a herald of the faith; if, without fuss, he shares and helps to sustain the life of the Church: then the orthodoxy of his opinions may be presumed until the contrary is conclusively proved. Whatever corrections or clarifications of his teaching may become necessary can safely be left to the work of theology itself and to the future. There is no need of an immediate threat of excommunication.

7

CHURCH OF CONCRETE DIRECTIVES

The Church today should have the courage for concrete imperatives and 'directives', even in regard to socio-political action by Christians in the world. In this respect the Church is now in a difficult situation. The really fundamental and permanent principles of Christian action, particularly in regard to secular society, were formerly taken for granted as involved in a unity together with concrete practices and the actualization of ideal types, in the light of which they were understood and realized. Thus in practice the proclamation of the general and permanent principles of Christian action was formerly by its nature a proclamation of concrete imperatives, since in fact it was impossible to realize the general principles except through these imperatives as proclaimed.

It is different today. The general principles both of so-called natural law and of a specifically Christian morality can now be realized concretely in a variety of ways: considerably diverse life-styles, considerably diverse types of society and economy, and so on, without any of these different types being able to be singled out as the only one which corresponds to Christian principles. In this way, however, the Christian principles which are authoritatively maintained and put forward as doctrine by the Church's *magisterium* become remarkably abstract and thus singularly ineffective. They are very often recognized as wholly right and yet seem so inept that we are left helpless when faced with a concrete choice between such ideal types. It is in the details that we seem to come up against God and the devil, but the Church seems to be proclaiming only generalities. In response to such concrete questions and the demand for clear imperatives for concrete action, the Church herself often explains that she is not competent here and has to leave these decisions to conscience and the expertise of individuals and particular groups; the latter with their secular expertise or with a prophetically charismatic inspiration must find for themselves the concrete expression of abstract Christian principles.

There is no doubt that the Church's *magisterium* properly speaking cannot get doctrinally beyond the sphere of abstract, theoretical (human and theological) reason, and of general principles. But, while observing this with relief or regret, we must also note immediately the qualification 'properly speaking': the *magisterium* as such. And the question may be raised whether the function of the institutional Church as a whole has to be restricted always and necessarily to this sphere of theoretical reason. It may be asked whether the institutional Church must really regard herself solely as the doctrinaire guardian and teacher of abstract principles which become ever increasingly abstract and are liable to carry within themselves the danger of a terrifying sterility, even though we will not and may not assert that they have no real meaning at all for practical life. If individual Christians and Christian groups in society, by their expertise and also (occasionally) in virtue of a charismatic inspiration, can go beyond the abstract principles to reach quite concrete imperatives and decisions, grasping in the concrete what is really to be done here and now, what is 'the will of God', there is really no reason why the same opportunity should be denied *a priori* to the institutional Church as such.

Of course she cannot put forward such imperatives and what I have called 'directives' magisterially as binding in faith. But if she cannot and may not do this (although she has certainly done it often enough), can she only be silent when Christians in concrete situations are evidently rightly convinced that the decision to be made by the Christian conscience is not completely indifferent and of no consequence, merely because several decisions are possible in the light of Christian theoretical reason and a particular decision cannot be conclusively deduced from Christian principles? What I mean is that it is open to the Church to proclaim also concrete imperatives both in the sphere of the Church's own life and in particular with reference to social policy and social criticism. For she has a 'pastoral office' and it is not obvious why what is really meant by the term cannot extend beyond the action of Christians within the narrower ecclesiastical sphere, beyond the 'commandments of the Church' properly so called.

By proclaiming such imperatives the Church is not teaching any eternal truths; she is not setting up any dogmas nor issuing any laws in the proper sense of the term. In this respect she appeals more to the expertise, to the capacity for critical discrimination, of the Christian conscience whose verdict theoretically cannot be completely nullified; she makes appeals which certainly leave decisions to the Christian conscience of the individual and of particular groups, but are nevertheless relevant to the formation of that conscience. I too have the spirit of Christ, said St Paul in a similar situation, not simply proclaiming any indisputable law and yet not being content to be merely silent. The Church could distinguish much more clearly the implications of such imperatives and directives for the Christian conscience of the individual from the binding character of the Church's official teaching properly so called. If it has now become clear to Christians in the Church—as it was not hitherto—that a concrete, historical decision cannot be justified in God's sight merely because it is not certainly and unambiguously in conflict with the theoretical principles of Christianity put forward by the Church's *magisterium* properly so called, that is not to say that such imperatives and directives are any less important. If Christians who are morally mature understand that a decision is not really concretely, historically appropriate and effective for the future and not therefore the will of God, merely because it cannot be absolutely certainly contested in the light of Christian theoretical reason, they can also become completely open and alert to imperatives and directives of the institutional Church: the latter, clearly recognized as such, can help them freely and conscientiously to make the really concretely right decision.

The Church does in fact proclaim such imperatives and directives. Not a little of what is of decisive importance—for example, in Paul VI's *Populorum progressio*—can certainly not be deduced as strictly logical conclusions from the Christian principles for human society; and yet it was proclaimed, and rightly. But if we had reflected in a more clearly theological way on the special character of these somewhat prophetical and not properly doctrinal imperatives and directives, and if Christians had been accustomed to take up the right attitude towards them, the Church in her office-holders would presumably more easily and more often find the courage for this sort of proclamation. It might be possible then to overcome the dilemma which seems to be involved here: that office-holders put forward either merely colourless principles which upset no one or what are supposed to be their own private opinions which, for that very reason, interest no one. The Church could be much more active in social criticism if she did not feel that she was always forced to choose between putting forward something as a matter of faith, requiring the assent of Christians to her official teaching, or of simply remaining silent. If the institutional Church more clearly and more often summoned up the courage (there will be sufficient opportunities today and in the future) for such imperatives and directives, there might perhaps be greater confusion in the Church, but there would be an end to that graveyard peace which very often prevails inside and outside of the Church, and in which—since theoretical reason claims to be alone legitimate and yet has nothing to say—the 'practical people' do whatever the whim of the moment suggests.

What has just been said remains very theoretical and general. The reason is that the concrete effectiveness of these imperatives and directives—which is all that really matters—can be achieved only if they are widely accepted by individual Christians and particular groups within the Church. But then the question arises of how the institutional Church can win the assent of her people to these imperatives and directives which go beyond the principles generally proclaimed. A preliminary requirement, as we have already suggested, is the training of the individual Christian's conscience. There is a further question as to how it can be made intelligible and palpable to ordinary Christians that such imperatives and directives are to be traced back through the office-holders to a higher expertise on the part of the Church or to a charismatic impulse from above and therefore may not be treated lightly from the start by individual Christians as if they were merely arbitrary opinions. Of course the Church can be wide of the mark in such imperatives and directives in a different way and more palpably than in theoretical declarations of the *magisterium*. But this is a risk that must be taken if the Church is not to seem merely pedantic, to be living in a world of pure theory, remote from life, making pronouncements that do not touch the stubborn concreteness of real life. What has been said holds—in varying degrees, of course—both of the Church as a whole in her supreme office and also of bishops' conferences and individual bishops.

With these imperatives and directives of course—particularly if they take the form of social criticism—any sort of small-mindedness or pedantry must be avoided. However little these imperatives can be derived purely theoretically from general principles alone, they must be seen clearly to emerge from the innermost centre of a committed Christian conscience, they must be put forward with prophetic force and therefore presuppose also office-holders who are capable of doing this, without having to cover themselves pedantically by referring to the paragraphs of Denzinger.* This sort of thing, of course, also presupposes an education which prevents Christians from losing trust in the institutional Church, even when their conscience does not permit them to apply these imperatives and directives to their own Christian action. Christians must be trained and educated to come to terms with the intrinsic pluralism involved in such a case; and even if these cases did not arise, the training would still be indispensable, since a certain pluralism of theoretical opinion simply cannot be avoided in the Church today.

The meaning of the concept of 'directive' perhaps still needs to be explained more precisely. Later on, a warning will be raised against making too much use of a doctrinaire casuistry in proclaiming doctrine today. It will be said that we must not attach too high a theological qualification to problematic dogmatic and moral teachings, merely in order not to disturb the so-called 'simple faithful', not to make them insecure and disturbed, to enable them to know exactly what they have to think and do. If then we speak of 'directives' here, we are not insisting on their possibilities and usefulness in order once more to justify that over-simplified proclamation against which we shall later be issuing a warning.

There is a 'directive' in our sense only if its specific theological 'qualification' is expressly stated, if it is in the form

---

* Henricus Denzinger, *Enchiridion Symbolorum, Definitionum et Declarationum de rebus fidei et morum.* A collection of church documents, first published in 1854 and continually brought up to date by a series of editors up to the present time, most recently by Adolf Schönmetzer. It is published by Herder, Freiburg-im-Breisgau, Germany.

of an imperative calling for the free historical decision of individuals and Christian groups, if it is not a piece of dogmatic or moral-theological casuistry but a creative appeal to those who have to create a particular, concrete future precisely out of several possibilities open to Christians. Such a directive therefore is *a priori* quite different from a dogma, to which a qualification in regard to its binding force is attached only cautiously and modestly on the level of theoretical reason and reflection. It would be of considerable significance if Christians of today and tomorrow were to become fully aware of the fact that a devotion of fundamental importance for the future could be involved in a doctrinally very problematic statement.

8

CHURCH OF REAL SPIRITUALITY

We really ought to have in the German Church something that might properly be called 'spirituality'. This does not mean that our Christian thought and life must be very exclusive and move within a very narrow space. This is impossible, if only because 'spirituality' not only includes love for our close or distant neighbour, but a love which today is obviously more than a private affair and takes the form of a real struggle for more justice and freedom in society; only then is it really Christian love and not an introverted cultivation of one's own precious soul.

This is presupposed and we shall return to it later. But now we have to point out that the Church must be a 'spiritual' Church if it is to remain true to its own nature. But this does not mean the mere rejection of an ultimately atheistic 'horizontalism', but first of all that the Church today must rediscover and bring into operation its own spiritual resources. If we are honest, we must admit that we are to a terrifying extent a spiritually lifeless Church. Living spirituality—which of course still exists today—has withdrawn in a singular way from the public life of the Church (considered sociologically) and has hidden in small conventicles of the remaining pious people. The Church's public life even today (for all the good will which is not to be questioned) is dominated to a terrifying extent by ritualism, legalism, administration, and a boring and resigned spiritual mediocrity continuing along familiar lines.

At this stage, I would like to make myself a little more clear. I regard myself too as one of the 'Church's officials', and I am not using the term in a pejorative sense. I am using it of myself and many others in this connection only in order to make clear that we priests and bishops, precisely in virtue of our calling, are continually programmed in advance and propped up by the assumptions of society which, together with the familiarity of our calling, the livelihood it secures, with the environment

in which we live, make Christianity easy—almost too easy—
for us. To these church officials I say (and thus of course I
am throwing a large stone also at my own glass house): Use
a little existential imagination and suppose that you are not
a church official, that you are earning your living as a dustman
or (if you prefer) as a biochemist working in a laboratory where
there is never a word about God all day and yet results are
obtained of which you can be proud. Imagine that your head
is weary from the clatter of dustbins or from molecular physics
and its mathematics. Imagine that this situation of yours were
to last more or less a whole lifetime and that you had not been
involved in it merely in the course of your missionary activity.
And now try to give these people in this environment the message of Christianity, try to preach Jesus' message of eternal
life. Listen how you tell it, judge for yourselves how it sounds,
reflect *how* you ought to tell it if it is not to be rejected as these
people might reject someone trying to talk about Tibetan
medicine. What would you say in these surroundings?

How, first of all, would you translate the word 'God'? How
would you speak of Jesus in such a way that another person
can get some idea of the importance he has in your life, his
real meaning for you, a meaning which is also relevant to the
life which these others lead? Would not many of the words
which we now hand out from the pulpit, unthinkingly, without
more ado, stick in our throats? Would you then be so quick
to refer to Denzinger? Would you talk so much and so stubbornly about things which you yourselves don't count as part
of the innermost core of your message? And so little about
things which a person must grasp first if he is to come to
believe today? Don't say that you are talking in the first place
to people who already believe. If the latter are not living just as
comfortably as you are in the vanishing mental situation of a
people's Church, they are equally threatened by that inability
to believe which you are not facing afresh, radically and boldly.
Don't say that you are not anyway in the situation in which you
ought to place yourselves with the aid of that existential imagination which every preacher needs today.

Certainly the situation in which we are in fact, in which we
still are, is also a grace of God, the concrete form of the grace
of faith which has been granted to us but not to the many others.

But it is a dangerous grace, a grace that can be abused by the kind of sloth and pettiness that is prevalent among Christians. And a preacher should pray for the grace of the existential imagination already mentioned, so that he can really preach in the way that is necessary today: slowly, cautiously, gently, groping step by step towards that reality for which he had hitherto always been ready with too many words; modestly and even disturbed as he realizes how difficult it is to attest real faith and not merely its historical and social objectivations and relics. Don't try to console when there is no scope for consolation. Don't 'solve' life's problems when their sole ultimate solution lies in God's incomprehensibility, his nature, and his freedom.

When preaching, don't forget that we human beings must all pass through a narrow way (called death), a thousand times narrower than the hole pierced by a laser beam, and we don't know—that is, we can't imagine—what there is in us that can really get through; that we are hoping against hope, consoled (how, we cannot say) in the midst of despair. Don't build on the fact that the 'heathens' too have their flower-children who are just as naïve as we Christians are, as long as all goes well and Vietnam and napalm bombs are far away. Remember that our listeners do indeed live their middle-class lives as satisfied members of the consumer society just as we do, are as assured as we are (until death comes, which we are allowed to face today only in aseptic hospitals where everybody abandons everybody else), but nevertheless are and remain distrustful when we base our preaching on these assumptions.

Have you ever once spoken in the joy of the Holy Spirit, in the light of the true, unvarnished situation (I am not saying how I would answer the question myself)? Admit it: are you not happy that for the most part no answer at all is expected of us in the light of the real situation, that we are allowed to talk again only at the graveside, with due solemnity, after the others have overcome their first shock and the scandal of the facts has been suppressed also among the heathens? Have you ever once experienced the terror that makes your heart stop when you hear yourself and when your pious and learned words sound even to yourself like an intolerable bla-bla? Have you ever really come once through this inferno?

Where are the tongues of fire talking of God and his love? Where do men speak of the 'commandments' of God, not as a duty to be painfully observed, but as the glorious liberation of man from the enslavement of mortal fear and frustrating egoism? Where in the Church do men not only pray but also experience prayer as the pentecostal gift of the Spirit, as glorious grace? Where, beyond all rational indoctrination of God's existence, is there an initiation into the mystery of that living experience which arises from the centre of our own existence? Where in the priests' seminaries are the ancient classics of the spiritual life read with the conviction that even today they still have something to tell us? Where is there an understanding of the logic of existential decision in which, over and above all purely 'objective' reasoning, a person asks about the will of God as it holds precisely for him and is every time unique? Where is the willingness to learn that all socio-critical and socio-political commitment—which today, in the form of a struggle for greater freedom and justice, is a sacred duty for Christians and the Church—contains or should contain within itself a secret spirituality, since for the Christian it grows out of that inner-most, absolute obligation which places man before God, whether he reflects on it or not?

Contemplative orders may find 'vocations' even today. But do we feel that these 'contemplatives' as such really belong to us, that they represent an attitude which simply must not be lacking in our life if we really want to be Christians: the atti-tude in which a person really accepts in adoration and love the ineffable mystery of his life in an act of renunciation, hopefully reaching out beyond all the possible goods that this life can offer to seize on the promise which has no name, accepting death as the victory and dawn of eternal life? Where then are there still the 'spiritual fathers', the Christian *gurus*, who possess the charisma of initiating into meditation and even into a mysticism in which man's ultimate reality—his union with God—is accepted in a holy courage? Where are the people who have the courage to be disciples of such spiritual fathers? Is it then really obvious that this master-disciple relationship exists only in a secularized form, in depth-psychology?

Let us admit, however, our impoverished spirituality in the German Church today. This poverty cannot be turned into riches merely by admitting it; nor do we know exactly what a richer spirituality of the future will look like in the concrete, particularly as it may also be the wealth of the poor who are longing for God's mercy. But such an admission of spiritual poverty in the private and public life of the Church might provide scope and a visible justification for the courage to seek a new spirituality, a spirituality which would not have to be excused as a relic from the Church's past, since without it the Church herself would become a relic from former times.

The Church then must remain the Church of mystery and of the evangelical joy of redeemed freedom. She may not be reduced to a humanitarian welfare association, if only because in the long run man cannot endure himself unless he is redeemed into the open freedom of God. Only when man knows that he is infinitely more than is immediately palpable—namely, the man of the infinite God of unlimited freedom and bliss—can he really endure himself in the long run. Otherwise he slowly stifles in his own finiteness and all lofty talk about man's dignity and duty comes to sound increasingly hollow. The Church therefore is concerned from first to last with God.

It is true that this word 'God' has been terribly misused. It is of course the least comprehensible of words. Its real content as the ineffable mystery, overtaxing man, never to be entered as a definite item in his life's accounts, must constantly be divined afresh and suffered through all the heights and depths of human experience. But this is how the Church must speak of God. Not in order to dispense herself and man from tasks which man himself most solve; not to keep at hand an opium of *that* people which itself sets up and fulfils its task and thus struggles for ever new and—if possible—greater freedom from self-alienation. There must be talk of God in order to give him glory. In this way and only in this way will the message of God be able to show its liberating power. But if God is known, hoped for and loved for his own sake, if he is glorified as the one who will give his blessed infiniteness in the grace of the Holy Spirit to man himself as his own, then man becomes truly a man of absolute hope against all hope, a man of ultimate freedom, who as such can live for others without any final reservation: in spite of all experience of his limitation and the sense of his own guilt, he can find that this world, which seems so desperately dark and seems constantly to make a mockery of our own ideals, is nevertheless good and can be accepted in a final trustfulness.

We talk too little about God in the Church or we talk about him in a dry, pedantic fashion, without any real vitality. We have learned too little of the incomprehensibly noble art of a true initiation into the mystery of experience of God and therefore also apply it far too little. That is why, in face of worldwide atheism, we have the feeling of being merely on the defensive. This impression—which in the very last resort is false—arises of course also to a large extent because we interpret the *mysterious* presence of God and its history, neither of which can obviously correspond to our expectations, as the absence of God or we even rig up a Death of God theology, not knowing at all what the word 'God' means.

If we speak of God as if he had to be a friend in need in our situations in life precisely in the way that we would like, then of course we can only admit that this God doesn't occur in the world and is presumably dead. But this God, who spares us the need of capitulation before his incomprehensibility in order to be saved, has never been the God of Christianity where this was rightly understood. But when man surrenders himself to the true God unconditionally in a final hope, beyond all calculable individual realities, he comes into his ultimate freedom which is filled with God himself and carries within itself a secret bliss even when in our despair we no longer cope with ourselves and this world.

As long as all this remains theory and we preach it as if it were merely a slick, Utopian ideology, on which people are careful not to rely in real life, the message of God of course does not redeem and liberate. We must take the risk of this message without reinsurance: then it shows that it sustains and liberates. Only when the message of the living God is preached in the churches with all the power of the Spirit, will the impression disappear that the Church is merely an odd relic from the age of a society doomed to decline. Only when we manage to grasp and make a part of our life the fact that God is not a projection which we slowly come to understand as such, but we ourselves are God's projection, set up in autonomy and freedom; only when we succeed in this by discovering guilelessly and trustingly that what is first and last in us has always secretly thought and lived in this way and that we can therefore also accept it in freedom: only then do we experience the liberating and saving power of the message of the living God, of his redeeming grace, of his forgiveness and of his deifying love which no longer raises any questions since it is itself the one answer.

In a Church of true spirituality one thing more must be vigorously proclaimed: Jesus. That is, the faith that in the history of our life and of the world the absolute self-utterance of God as of life liberating us has been made firm for ever in him: in him who was given up in death, who was finally accepted by God and who lives.

When proclaiming this Jesus as him who in this sense is our Lord, certain things must be made clear. On the one hand, in this starting point for a Christian understanding of Jesus by faith the whole traditional and still binding Christology is involved; on the other hand, if it is to be really intelligible and credible, this Christology cannot be summed up purely and simply in a statement of 'Christology of descent', 'from above', but must begin with the experience of Jesus who obediently accepted in a radical love for God and men the breakdown of his life and his mission *and* just so became credible as the one finally assumed into God's life *and* thus became for us the unsurpassable word of God's self-utterance to us. This is not the place to show that the Christology taught by the Church and permanently binding can be reached from this starting point and also understood in its true sense. It should however be emphasized that there can be and is a common confession by Christians of Jesus Christ prior to many christological statements which are part of the Church's official teaching but difficult for many people today to understand.

If on the one hand we start out from this most primitive and in a sense still premetaphysical Christology and obtain a common agreement on it and on the other hand manage to get Christians who are allergic to metaphysical formulations of Christology at least to have an open mind in regard to the Church's traditional formularies, then a very broad (and this does not mean merely general) consensus might be attained among those who are willing to call themselves Christians. And in turn the profession of faith in Jesus as Christ and Lord, the decisive and final word of God in history might become more alive, more joyous and spontaneous.

Through this two-in-one profession of faith in God and in Jesus, the word of God's self-utterance in history, the Church can and must be, remain, and become more and more the Church of the mystery and evangelical joy of redeemed freedom: a Church of true spirituality.

PART THREE

How can a Church of the Future be Conceived?

In the third part of our reflections we ask: How can a Church of the future be conceived? In view of the openness of the future and the impossibility of planning it, this question in the last resort is obviously unanswerable. This third part is distinguished from the second in as much as we are now looking to a rather more distant future, not only stating requirements which are directly relevant at all times, but also trying to anticipate some things which certainly cannot be realized overnight but for which we ought to prepare the way with resolution and foresight. At the same time, it is inevitable that something of what is to be said now has already been briefly discussed in the second part; on the other hand, any discussion of the requirements for a more distant future has also its importance for the present.

Any attempt at concrete answers to our third question will inevitably involve some repetition of what was said in the second part. This may even be useful. With such answers we need not worry too much whether they are mainly formal or mainly material in their content, whether therefore they demand primarily an attitude or a concrete object.

1

OPEN CHURCH

In future we must take the risk, not only of a Church with 'open doors', but of an 'open Church'. We cannot remain in the ghetto nor may we return to it. Anyone who experiences and endures the confusion, partly unavoidable, partly avoidable, in all dimensions of teaching and practice, which undoubtedly exists in the Church, is certainly tempted to long for the Church which older people among us knew under the four Pius's and up to the last Council. We are then tempted, in such movements as that 'for Pope and Church', in what is in fact in the last resort a sterile pseudo-orthodoxy, to 'purify' the Church as rapidly as possible and by administrative measures to draw clear frontiers, to 'restore' the old order: in a word to enter on the march into the ghetto, even though the Church would then become, not the 'little flock' of the gospel, but really a sect with a ghetto mentality.

Of course no serious churchman will defend such a march into the ghetto explicitly in the form of a thesis. But there is sufficient evidence of an unreflecting ghetto mentality in our midst which, without an explicit doctrine, is trying to save clarity, order, piety, and orthodoxy by giving the Church a form which in terms of sociology of religion and political ideas is that of a sect. This sort of sect exists when the far greater majority of such a social group in practice or intentionally withdraws from the public life of society, continues only to protest, only to see around itself a world given up to evil. The members of this sectarian group, at least *as* members, are no longer interested in objectives and tasks in the present world; their life-style is maintained by as many taboos as possible; every attempt is made to provide within the sect for as many of life's needs as still have to be satisfied. All those who do not belong to the group are regarded as obviously more or less dangerous enemies. The members know always and in every case precisely which political party they must vote for; they assume (of course, without admitting it) that an answer has to be ready for every question that might arise in the future. They know exactly— for instance—what in literature and art is adapted to Christian sensitivity and what is not; they react from the very beginning and more or less solely from a moral standpoint (or what they regard as a moral standpoint) to expressions of the cultural life of society. They are hypersensitive to criticism within their own ranks and particularly to criticism of office-holders, calling far too quickly and too readily for solidarity in order to stand up to the 'enemies'. If the Church is not to become to some extent a sect of this kind, it must become and remain an open Church.

First of all, the Church must be open even in regard to orthodoxy. Because of the importance of the matter, I may be permitted to take up again a theme already mentioned. Of course for a member of the Church there is in principle and as such teaching that is binding in faith. Of course the Church can and must speak an unambiguous language when one of her dogmas is publicly denied or dismissed as unimportant and must forcefully repel heresy in her midst. But on this two things must be said at once.

In the first place, when frontiers are drawn in this way, it must be a question of real dogmas or—which is quite possible —if defensive measures are considered necessary against dangers to orthodoxy, it must also be expressly stated what is involved: in other words, the theological qualification of such a declaration must be clearly affixed.

It is not so easy to say exactly what many good Christians think is meant by the word 'God'. It is possible to repeat orthodox formulas of Christology, to feel too self-assured as orthodox, and yet only to have repeated what for many people of today are empty formulas, people to whom it would be quite possible to convey an understanding of the Christian profession of faith in Jesus. Certainly the decisive thing about Jesus Christ is not conveyed merely by pointing out lyrically or stubbornly that he ate with tax-collectors and prostitutes, but at the same time it cannot be said that this fact means nothing to us today. It is not so easy to say exactly when a theology of the unity of the love of God and neighbour really leads only to God being supplanted by man alone. It needs to be said that the commandment of the Church (and only of the Church) of annual confession binds only those who are conscious of a subjectively grave sin, nor has anyone the right to claim as certain that this guilt-situation is normal in the life of Christians. It cannot be asserted that a ruling on the co-operation of the laity in official decision-making is always and in every case contrary to the constitutional law of the Church merely because the acceptance of this co-operation and consent is binding on office-holders. It cannot be said that it is *a priori* impossible for the prevailing administrative law in the Church to exhibit also features of an unchristian and inhuman character. It is not *a priori* unchristian and impious to ask whether the Church's legislation on celibacy may not be changed and even must be changed in the light of the pastoral situation of the Church in the future.

It is not a dogma that a service of penance cannot have any sacramental character. It is not absolutely certain where the frontiers for an open communion lie. It is not clear that divorced people who remarry after a first, sacramental marriage can in *no* circumstances be admitted to the sacraments as long as they stand by the second marriage as such. The Sunday obligation cannot be pressed as if it had been proclaimed at Sinai as divine law, valid forever. Nor is it so clear, as people sometimes think, what are the possibilities even for a Christian conscience in regard to the *state's* penal laws against termination of pregnancy. Since no political party in practice is so completely Christian in each and every respect and since a party may act very gently as a result of being deeply involved in sins of omission and yet in reality in a very solidly unchristian way, it is not so easy to say when a party can no longer rely on the support of Christians and Catholics.

The courage publicly to define very clearly the frontiers at which real heresies start in the Church must be coupled with a very exact and self-critical reflection as to *where* there is real heresy and where the Church can really require the Catholic to decide against it.

There is a second point. When authority in the Church fulfils its function and duty, speaking out clearly against a real heresy, the declaration is in most cases ineffective in practice: the decision therefore should not merely appeal to the formal teaching authority of the Church's *magisterium* (legitimate in itself), but should obviously be made in the power of the living Spirit of faith, striving to substantiate the particular dogma from the innermost centre of Christian faith. Otherwise declarations of this kind put too great a strain on the formal teaching authority of the *magisterium* and remain ineffective, since in fact, in the minds of those to whom they are addressed, the binding authority of the *magisterium* is by no means so unassailably certain, but is just as much under threat as the particular dogma that has to be defended. Unless it is substantiated vigorously from those basic convictions which are still shared by the people addressed, the very defence of the dogma itself becomes for them an argument against the teaching authority of the Church in general.

Beyond this, however, something must be said to explain how we can talk of an open Church, while still maintaining the unambiguous 'orthodoxy' of the Church as it exists in the concrete today. We have to go beyond the familiar distinction between public and secret heresy, which is hardly practicable any longer, and consider in terms of pastoral care and pastoral theology the fact that many Christians and Catholics living in their Church and attaching importance to this simply cannot be completely prevented—in view of the present-day intellectual pluralism and the over-abundant supply of material thrust into consciousness—from having opinions which are objectively heretical; we must remember also that these Christians and Catholics have a relationship with the Church's *magisterium* and authority which does not correspond to the fundamental requirements of the official understanding of the Church and of church-membership, but implies only a partial identification with the Church. Today, measured by the Church's teaching which is binding in principle, there are heresies within the Church, accepted in practice and also expressly stated by people who have no wish to leave the Church and in practice cannot be pinned down on their heresies (by excommunication and other measures).

For the social and psychological reasons just indicated, it is simply impossible in practice to eradicate these heresies existing within the Church. They present the Church's authority and the clergy with problems which formerly hardly existed at all and particularly not to this extent nor in this strength.

Ecclesiastical authority in the measures it adopts must first of all coolly recognize and allow for the impossibility of solving these problems, even though this does not imply any positive approval of this state of affairs: the average man in today's mental climate will not succeed in forming an outlook which is objectively free from heresy. Merely to appeal to a *fides implicita* does not help, since its presupposition—a determination in principle to adjust one's own conviction in every case unconditionally to the Church's official teaching—is equally imperilled.

The average man today does not permit himself *in practice* to be faced by the Church's authority with an either-or: to abandon these 'heresies' unconditionally or, if not simply to leave the Church, to regard himself as separated from her inwardly (theologically), even though not in terms of sociology of religion or citizenship. It is impossible in practice logically and humanly to reconcile with one another all the ideas floating in the consciousness of theologically uneducated-educated people today (and all are becoming educated in some sense) and to resolve all contradictions between them, since these ideas today have become too numerous and too complex to be wholly mastered. The normal man today therefore will simply not be able to realize such an either-or required of him by the Church's authority, no matter how objectively real the dilemma may be.

Before drawing from this fact the conclusion that really interests us, two observations may be permitted. First of all, these opinions deviating from objective dogma which exist in the minds of most members of the Church are not always and necessarily firm convictions, freely accepted, which alone can properly be called heresy, but merely views held temporarily and not regarded as final or absolute. Opinions of this kind, on the part even of normal people, must really be taken for granted in the current intellectual climate, since we are living in an age of the formation of scientific hypotheses, of opinions in various fields of learning accepted until revoked: an age when real victories consist in recognizing the falsity of opinions hitherto accepted as hypotheses and not so much in establishing the correctness of a new opinion. Opinions so understood and accepted in life however are not really (logically and existentially) in *heretical* opposition to the act of faith properly so-called and to its content, as long as there is an absolute commitment to the real substance of Christian faith, on which of course no further reflection is necessary.

Secondly, those who are authorized to explain the Church's official teaching can point out to such people that it is at least imprudent to assert too apodeictically an opinion which office-holders and theologians regard as not objectively compatible with dogma; they can suggest that it is better to consider this opinion in the same way as opinions are considered in other fields—as provisional, eventually conceivable, but still far from certain—and that it may be left to its fate as a part of the individual's progress in truth; meanwhile he may continue to entertain the sincere hope that the positive reconciliation, not yet possible, may come about eventually between the Church's official teaching (which he perhaps does not properly understand here and now) and his own opinion formulated provisionally and with some reservation in view of the possibility of a better understanding.

From all this we can see how difficult it is today theologically to assign exactly the limits of orthodoxy on the part of members of the Church, how there are circumstances in the religious life of the individual in the Church which will have to be considered again in connection with the theme of ecumenism. Theologically, it is not so easy to say who is concretely and 'subjectively' really in the Church by his faith and who is not. In the light of this alone the Church is an open Church, whether she wants to be or not, whether she reflects on it or not, or simplifies the situation and thus overlooks it.

If we remember that there are presumably very many people like those we have just been considering, who do not belong to the Church in terms of sociology of religion or of citizenship and yet have the outlook involved in a positive relationship to the Church together with a merely partial identification with her, then it becomes still more clear how difficult it is to establish precisely where is the door of the Church in a theological and not merely ecclesial-sociological sense, who is inside and who is outside. We have already insisted that we are by no means denying a certain theological significance even to civic and ecclesial-sociological membership of the Church. But because the latter alone does not constitute full membership of the Church and because—in a theological sense—it is of considerably less significance than the other constitutive elements (baptism, complete faith, state of grace, complete self-identification with the Church), we may not even in *practice* act as if Catholics and non-Catholics were to be distinguished from one another in regard to membership of the Church solely by this ecclesial-sociological factor.

What do these reflections mean in practice? First of all, the Church in her proclamation must always be making new efforts to incorporate fully those who do not yet belong completely to the Church, even though we generally regard them as such because they are 'practising'. This is a task that can never be completely and finally accomplished in practice today. Behind the proclamation there must be a clear and unbiased understanding of those to whom it is addressed. There need not and should not, of course, be an explicit mention every time of this intention. That would be stupid and boring. But the preacher must be clearly aware of what his sermon really presupposes in his hearer. In the treatment of a definite, restricted dogmatic or moral theme, for example, he cannot appeal merely to the authority of the Church's *magisterium* in order to produce clarity and certainty, since his hearers are Catholic anyway and therefore recognize this authority. The fact is that any treatment of a particular theme of this kind must draw its arguments from the Christian's ultimate, basic convictions which, it can be presumed, are held by the listeners; the same arguments must be used constantly to establish and defend the formal teaching authority of the Church itself, even when it stands up for the doctrine in question.

In future, without prejudice and without too much anxiety about dogma, we should count the 'sympathizers' around the Church in practice as belonging to her and let them see this from our whole attitude, without of course wanting simply to 'take them in' or giving them the impression that this is our aim. In practice this means that we can quietly and benevolently tolerate a perceptible or public expression of these 'sympathizers' to the effect that they can only partly identify themselves with the Church or even with Christianity. At the same time of course we must be aware of the concrete results of such a practice, while not being too much afraid of them, simply because now and in the future they can no longer be avoided.

This means—to take a concrete example—that the Catholic Church in future will make on us, who are old and settled in our ways, an impression in the dimension of ecclesial empiricism similar to that which we had formerly—partly correctly, but also with some exaggeration—of the Evangelical Church: we thought it was possible there to say and express in public more or less anything one wanted to say. We certainly need not fear that we shall have too much of this sort of confusion in the future. This is simply because people who have really decided against Christianity will of themselves get well away from the Church and there is no reason to fear that an ultimately unchristian outside-opposition* will attempt or be able to infiltrate the Church and radically change its functions to any considerable degree. Nevertheless, concretely and practically, a pluralism will exist in the Church in the future and will find expression which cannot simply be recognized as legitimate in accordance with the strict dogmatic norms of the institutional Church in the same way as a legitimate pluralism of schools of theology with equal rights is accepted.

A pluralism in this sense, the constituents of which do not enjoy equal rights dogmatically speaking but do in fact exist in an open Church, need not threaten the real foundations of a dogmatically firm and self-assured Church. For there is within the Church an office which guards, fosters and always defends the whole content of Christian faith, without at every turn simply having to silence voices inside and outside the Church opposing or threatening this teaching. As we have shown, this is not only impossible in practice today, but would be tactically and from the missionary standpoint imprudent, since it would merely prevent many people who at present can only achieve a partial identification from slowly coming to a fuller self-identification with the Church and her faith. To take an example: there is no point in giving a person who is now in touch with the Church, but has some reservations, the impression at every moment that he is really only a tolerated 'guest'

---

* APO = *Ausserparlamentarische Opposition*, currently used of those who attempt to storm the parliamentary and other formerly exclusive orthodox bastions.

and not a full member of this believing community and society. Of course it is only through bold practice and impartially undertaken experiments that we can see how this sort of thing looks in a Church which is open and yet cannot be a kind of supermarket where everything is sold and anybody can buy.

2

ECUMENICAL CHURCH

We must be a Church with an honestly ecumenical objective. This is obvious and does not need to be substantiated at length after the Second Vatican Council. All that can be offered here therefore are some secondary observations on the theme which, as such, may well be to some extent subjective.

First of all, we should not underestimate what has already been achieved in the Ecumenical Movement. The Christian Churches are admittedly still divided, but it is extraordinary how much has been achieved in the last decades when we compare the present relations between the Churches with the situation as it was up to our own times. Of course the real unification of these Churches still remains a distant goal and an inescapable task of all Christians. But, if we look to that unity which is within the historical possibilities open to us (and as Christians we should not dismiss the ecumenical task all-too-easily by asserting that a realistic estimate of the situation simply does not reveal such concrete possibilities of a real unity), it would not be so very different in practice from the situation we have already reached. But this only proves how much has already been really achieved. For, in a pluralistic society embracing the whole world, the real possibilities within our horizon do not include bringing all those interested in Christianity, who are baptized and call themselves Christians, institutionally into one and the same Church.

Even if the large institutional Churches are to or may unite with one another, it can be assumed that many Christians will remain outside this unity for which we are striving and which as such can be achieved. The reasons for this may be theological or religio-sociological. Furthermore, even this unity of the Churches which is being sought and is really possible will be much more pluralistic in character, both theologically and institutionally, than what we have hitherto known, at least up to recent times and in the Catholic Church. This holds even when we are sure and want to maintain that the one Church we are seeking cannot come to be as a result of arbitrarily reducing the number of Catholic dogmas, but only through a really forward-looking fresh understanding of the whole substance of Catholic dogma and a lively discussion on the part of all the Churches in their common world-wide developing mental and social situation: a discussion which will become more and more urgent for the future.

If, however, we understand realistically a possible unity of the Churches, allowing for these restrictions and peculiarities, then it has not yet been attained and it remains an urgent task; but it is not quite so remote from the present state of the *oikoumene* as we Catholics are tempted to think when we regard the attainment of unity simply as a quantitative enlargement of the Catholic Church through the incorporation of other Churches into ours. A realistic estimate of the unity which can be achieved is not very different in practice from the relationship which now exists between the Churches as a result of ecumenical efforts. This is not always appreciated because people overlook the fact that the future Church will in any case be much more pluralistic than our Church has palpably been juridically and in terms of sociology of religion since the Reformation period.

This really means even now that a unity of the exact nature to which we were accustomed neither can nor should be sought, since it can neither be achieved nor really be required in the light of Catholic dogma. A really possible union of the Churches is in any case not the same as an increase in the number of individual conversions to the Church. Should we then be content with the present state of affairs, aiming only at a further expansion of what has already been achieved? Is it sufficient to maintain the present friendly and respectful attitude of the Churches to one another and to co-operate even more—intensively and extensively—in the struggle for justice, freedom, and human dignity in the world? Certainly not. But how are we really to make further progress?

If we leave aside the question of the papacy—which will be dealt with in another context—and if we do not require in practice the assent of all Christians to a profession of faith or a theology of the one Church of the future, thus leaving no one outside that Church, then it seems to me that there are no further obstacles of a theological or confessional character to divide the denominations. But this sort of theological progress, attained or within reach, in itself has hitherto produced little or no results by way of Church-union. Nor does it seem very realistic to expect that such progress towards a theological consensus in the future to do much for a real unity of the Churches. There are various reasons for this.

In the Orthodox and Evangelical Churches it is scarcely possible to look to an official and institutional authority interested in this theological progress and able to embody its results in concrete decisions to promote Church-union. In the Catholic Church hitherto we have not been able to get round to making official and concrete suggestions for possible changes in the institutional character of the Church of the future which would also be acceptable in our own institutional but changeable situation. In addition, we start out more or less everywhere from the tacit assumption that absolutely all or almost all Christians, who belong to one or the other Church or Christian community, will be brought into this one Church of the future: and this of course makes the task simply impossible. What then can we seriously hope for in the reasonably foreseeable future?

I may be allowed to make a suggestion for a goal of the Ecumenical Movement which to most people may seem absolutely Utopian and for most Catholic theologians certainly not compatible with Catholic dogma. For there is an obligation on all Christians to strive for the unity of the Church which cannot simply be postponed till the Last Day, and yet it can scarcely be denied that the Ecumenical Movement seems to be stagnating (apart from a more intense co-operation of the Churches in the service of the world). Most Christians are preoccupied with their internal difficulties and almost absorbed by these and thus not a few churchmen may even find this stagnation by no means undesirable. In view of all this, an apparently Utopian suggestion may be made.

Hitherto (apart from improving relations and co-operating in social projects) we have tried to tackle the question of union from the theological and confessional aspect and regarded institutional unification purely as a consequence of this settlement of controversial theological issues. Would it not perhaps be possible to proceed in the opposite direction? Could we not consider full unity of faith and theology as a consequence of institutional unification, particularly since the latter need not mean institutional uniformity based on dogma as hitherto envisaged by the Code of Canon Law?

If we want to consider this question, we must first start out from a fact which of course requires more theological interpretation; even in the Catholic Church there is a considerable difference between the faith as known and accepted in practice by the majority of Catholics and the teaching of the institutional Church with its subtle nuances. Hence a large number of Christians in all denominations think that they can perceive a unity in what is really and not merely officially believed. If then the Churches were to unite institutionally in a way that is now possible and acceptable even for a strict, dogmatic Catholic conscience, the new awareness of faith would scarcely differ from the old, even in that part of the new Church which stemmed from the Roman Catholic Church. This would remain so at least as long as no attempt were made to want to keep even the 'very liberal' Christians within the institution, but only to unite institutionally those Christians in all Churches who believe in Christ as God and Redeemer (in the sense understood by the World Council of Churches).

But how could the Petrine ministry be introduced into such a Church? While allowing for the fact that the Churches entering into this unity would retain a relatively large juridical autonomy, we may reasonably assume that they would admit a certain function for the Petrine ministry. We may assume on the other hand that also in the Catholic Church alone *de facto* (even though not *de jure*) the future function of the papacy would be related to the maintenance of the unity of the Church, while allowing considerable autonomy to the constituent Churches, and to a decisive and vigorous defence of the basic substance of the Christian faith (without any really new dogmatic definitions). In the developing mentality of the future this is all that will be possible, but it will still be an enormously great and significant function. This papacy could be incorporated into the institutionally one Church and then could undertake the tasks of which it was *really* capable, without being opposed by the formerly Evangelical and Orthodox partial Churches but while continuing to be understood by the formerly

Roman Catholic partial Churches as they had always understood it. *This* understanding could not be *positively* required
of the formerly Orthodox or Evangelical partial Churches, even
though it would not be permissible for them officially *directly*
to *deny* it (which of course is not necessarily required by an
evangelical conscience of many or most Christians of these
Churches).

Keeping all this in mind, it seems to me that even a Catholic
might leave to the historical evolution of the total consciousness
of faith of this institutionally united Church the question whether
and how a positive reception of the whole, explicit dogma of the
Catholic Church might come about. In this respect, we simply
cannot expect everything to emerge from a dogmatic basis. This
is clear from our starting point: that many or most Catholics
do not explicitly grasp by faith all that belongs to the Catholic
Church's official understanding of faith and the Church.

Formerly people simply tacitly (rightly or wrongly) ascribed
to the individual member of a Church the faith which prevailed
and determined public consciousness in a denominationally homogeneous region. For that reason they could not see and appreciate
clearly enough this distance between the official and the actual
consciousness of faith within a Church (which cannot be bridged
over merely by appealing to a *fides implicita*), nor could they
even ask precisely about its theological implications or its
possible consequences for the institutional aspect of a Church.

If the idea of seeking institutional unity before dogmatic
unity is not purely Utopian and bound of its nature to break
down in face of the Catholic consciousness of faith, if it can
be recognized as theologically possible, the rigidity of the
institutions and their representatives in the particular Churches
is not thereby overcome. But, as these representatives can no
longer point to controversial theological issues as an obstacle
to unity, they may be asked whether they really wish to make
the contribution that is now possible to the unification of the
Churches or merely to indulge in polite ecumenical conver-
sation with one another, while in practice leaving everything as
it used to be.

If anyone can bring forward better questions and suggestions
for overcoming palpably the present stagnation in ecumenical
work, let him do so. It is to be hoped that there are better and

really practical suggestions. But if they are not forthcoming, the suggestion made here should be considered, so that the stagnation in ecumenism which undoubtedly exists today may be overcome at least in the long run. In any case, it seems to me, the initiative in this question must pass from the theologians to the office-holders. Admittedly the theologians have not yet completely fulfilled their task in this respect, but real progress even for them will only be possible after the office-holders have got to work on the more strictly institutional problems.

All this of course is far from being an exhaustive treatment of the ecumenical theme. But if this movement is to continue, without taking steps that have not been thoroughly and radically considered and which in the long run would not take us further but would only land us with a third denomination, no more alive and with even less Christian substance than the previous denominational Churches, then office-holders in all Churches must seriously consider how they are leading this movement itself to results which even the average, ordinary Christian can recognize as steps of this kind.

3

CHURCH FROM THE ROOTS

The Church of the future will be one built from below by basic communities as a result of free initiative and association. We should make every effort not to hold up, but to promote this development and direct it on to the right lines. To understand what this means, we must recall what was said in the first part of these reflections: concretely and socially, the Church will no longer exist as formerly through the mere persistence of her office, of her socially firm structures, and through an awareness of being taken for granted by public opinion, recruiting new members simply because the children adopt and maintain the life-style of their parents and are baptized and indoctrinated by the Church. The Church will exist only by being constantly renewed by a free decision of faith and the formation of congregations on the part of individuals in the midst of a secular society bearing no imprint of Christianity.

The fact that this is—at least from certain aspects—more a social than a theological description of the Church's constant renewal, that this renewal always involves accepting and recognizing the traditional message of the gospel and office coming from Christ through apostolic succession, all this in no way changes the new form in which the Church will exist today and in the future as compared with the past. Moreover, faith is always a freely and personally activated decision and therefore it cannot be contrary to the Church's nature to be more clearly visible than formerly as a social reality: for the Church cannot be a real factor in history except as sustained by this faith on the part of human beings.

Today of course the question is obscure and largely unanswered as to how the basic communities will in fact emerge from below, even though it will be through the call of the gospel and the message of the Church coming out of the past, and what they will look like in practice. Here and now we cannot and may not of course simply abolish the existing parishes spread out evenly, territorially, almost like police-stations. This would be wrong, particularly since such concrete parishes even today, with their concrete structures and vitality, may possibly come close to the basic communities as envisaged here or at least have a chance of becoming such. But parishes in the sense of administrative areas of the institutional Church, caring for people from above, are not the basic communities out of which the Church will have to be built up from below in the future. It is clear for theological reasons and in the light of the testimony of history that parishes constituted by a particular territory simply could not be the sole basic elements of the Church.

When living Christian communities are formed by the Christians themselves, when they possess and attain a certain structure, solidity, and permanence, they have just as much right as a territorial parish to be recognized as a basic element of the Church, as a Church of the bishop's Church and of the whole Church, even though their concrete basis of association is not a territory marked out by the diocesan authorities and simply including the Christians resident there. Of course a basic community has grown to more than a group of sympathizers, more than a small association of a few Christians, and become a basic element of the Church—a local Church—as the parish used or at least wanted to be and for the most part only the parish (apart from communities of religious and similar groups), only when it can really sustain the essential, basic functions of the Church (organized proclamation of the gospel, administration of the sacraments, Christian charity and so on) and can be taken for granted as the place of the constantly renewed eucharistic celebration.

When, however, *such* a community exists, coming from below, formed through the free decision of faith of its members, it has the right to be recognized as Church by the episcopal great Church and to have its community leader recognized by the great Church through ordination, as long as he can fulfil the necessary functions. Unquestionably the episcopal great Church has to test such a community leader in regard to his suitability; it may or even must train suitable people for these functions and offer them to these congregations. But this is not to say that the leader of such a basic community of the future must be simply and solely the appointed representative of the episcopal great Church and cannot be conceived otherwise.

It is quite compatible with the nature of the hierarchically constituted Catholic Church as a whole for such a basic community to present to the bishop a suitable leader coming from their midst and expect for the latter a relative* ordination and recognition for this particular community as a legal right. The qualities and conditions required for such a full community leader (also as leader of the Eucharist) cannot be decided in the light of our ideas of an all-round priestly office-holder who could carry out his duties everywhere and also exercise functions going far beyond those of a president of a smaller basic community; they must be seen as related to this basic community and the requirements of its leadership in the concrete situation. These demands can vary greatly with the particular situation of such a congregation, its secular social structure, its educational level, the concrete focal points of its life. We can set aside without hesitation the express or tacit assumption that someone can be leader in a Christian community appointed in virtue of his ordination (a 'priestly' leader), only if he can exercise this function successfully—at least in principle—anywhere at all, without regard to the particular community. The priest as leader of a local Christian community does not need to be regarded as a mobile state-official who is moved, promoted, acts as representative of a state which confronts a particular group of human beings as an alien factor armed with power, and alone 'organizes' them.

If the Church in a concrete situation cannot find a sufficient number of priestly congregational leaders who are bound to celibacy, it is obvious and requires no further theological discussion that the obligation of celibacy must not be imposed. We do not have to discuss here whether the conditions for giving up celibacy already exist in Germany; still less do we have to examine the more comprehensive question as to whether the traditional, legal bond between priesthood and celibacy is legitimate in itself for other reasons or may be called in question. But if a parish in the traditional sense cannot in practice fulfil

---

* Relative ordination: ordination with assignment to a particular congregation or church. Absolute ordination (the general practice today) is without such assignment.

the task required for the people of such a basic community of the future and particularly if an ordained priest cannot be appointed by the diocese, then—provided that the conditions for a Christian basic community are fulfilled—it is obvious that the community may present to the bishop a leader who comes from among themselves and has the necessary qualities for leadership and that he rightly receives ordination, even if he is married. *Salus animarum suprema lex.*

Such basic communities obviously have a duty to maintain unity with the episcopal great Church; they must also be constituted as members of the great Church, even if this means that they alone have to make certain 'sacrifices' and renounce some privileges; they have to observe laws of the whole Church which are rightly imposed and can be fulfilled in practice; despite their theological singularity, they must not try to develop any sectarian or heretical theology of their own; they must remain open in a self-critical spirit, in truth and love, to the life of the whole Church and also make practical contributions beyond their own frontiers; their singularity must not be so extreme that certain necessary functions, the fulfilment of which is under the supervision of the episcopal Church, simply cease or are curtailed. But all this does not exclude the fact that a basic community has its own pronounced character, gives itself a certain structure and (if you like to use the term) constitution, that it really demands from its freely associated members something which goes completely beyond what a parishioner today has to do for the ordinary parish.

The 'constitution' of such a basic community can certainly vary considerably in particular cases. The sustaining function and 'right of co-determination' of the laity may be considerably greater there than the general participation to which we have hitherto been accustomed, even though of course the apparently very 'authoritarian' official structures often concealed a much greater right of the laity in the parish to share in discussions: this alone shows that there is no reason for not giving legal recognition to something that often exists already in fact. The exact relationship therefore of the ordained leader of the community's eucharistic celebration to the rest of the members has a wide scope, but we must stick firmly to the principle that the ordained leader of the eucharistic celebration and the community leader as such have to be one and the same person and therefore the former cannot simply be a subordinate functionary for the liturgical acts in the congregation: he is not a kind of spiritual employee like the priest in the medieval 'autonomous' Church (*Eigenkirche*) under his feudal landlord. To place the ordained priest in such a position would be contrary to the spiritual and not merely secular-sociological nature of a Christian community and to the central importance of the eucharistic celebration in that congregation. We need not discuss this at greater length here.

The legitimate leadership of the eucharistic celebration and of the administration of the sacraments must in fact be held by one individual who is officially appointed to it, *rite vocatus*, and is not simply indiscriminately and casually always and in every case the affair of each and all. In this connection we can leave undecided the theological question whether, in an extreme emergency, a lay person—that is, someone not 'appointed' in principle for every case and at least for a long time—can exercise such a function. The theory that the leader of the eucharistic celebration and the community leader need not, or even should not, in principle be identical leads in practice to the eventual decline of the community and to an unchristian neglect of the sacramental element in the Church.

To defend this identity does not imply any clericalism. What we have to understand is that the principle, eucharistic-leader = community leader, can and must be taken just as seriously when read the other way round. Let us suppose that a community leader really undertakes all essential spiritual and not merely civic administrative functions (preaching, responsibility for a vigorous Christianity in a social group, practical charity, and so on) intensively enough and in a sense 'full time' (not precisely as occupying all his working hours, but in the sense of a personal and continuing commitment); let us suppose also that he has the necessary qualities and produces evidence of the requisite accomplishments and is thus to a certain extent different from the rest of the members of the congregation and for this very reason enjoys their trust. This is a person who should also be leader of this community's eucharistic celebration, since this corresponds to his other functions in this community and he should be recognized and appointed to this sacramental function also by ordination on the part of the episcopal great Church.

The concrete function and in fact as related to a particular community is *logically* prior to the official appointment to such a function, even if appointment—'priestly ordination'—is required for its normal exercise. If we see this clearly and unemotionally, then even the requirement of an identity between the leader of the eucharistic celebration and the community leader does not involve any danger of a false clericalism. If we leave aside the question of the concrete form required for the 'validity' of the conferring of legitimate community leadership, then we may say that in all the more important Christian Churches community leadership in a specifically Christian sense, going beyond civil administrative functions, is at least normally identical with leadership at the eucharistic celebration.

While accepting this principle, as we have said, the exact relationship of rights and duties between the priestly community leader on the one hand and the congregation with the rest of its necessary and legitimate functionaries on the other may vary considerably. Nor does the principle exclude the possibility of the existence in the congregation, among the so-called laity, of strong charismatic personalities who must be respected as such by the official leader and who exercise on the congregation, outside the juridical dimension, an influence greater than that which he in fact possesses. However desirable it might be for the official community leader himself to possess charismatically powers beyond the ordinary, it is simply impossible in every case for leadership and outstanding charismatic powers to be united in the one person. To demand it would be contrary to the freedom of God's Spirit in the Church and would necessarily lead to a perversion of the charismatic element. A certain discrepancy between what is socially established and the charismatic element is in the long run a blessing for the Church, prevents a fanatical subjectivizing of the Church which is intolerable in the long run, and must be accepted by Christians with the realism of hope and patience, even looking forward to the future, even though the discrepancy can never be completely overcome. Thus charismatic gifts may also be one of the qualities which commend a person for leadership in a basic community.

In this connection of course the question might be raised whether today or at least tomorrow, in the light of the secular social situation, a woman could be considered just as much as a man for leadership of a basic community and therefore could be ordained to the priestly office. Having in mind the society of today and even more of tomorrow, I see no reason in principle to give a negative answer to this question. On the other hand, this does not mean that in former social situations also women ought always to have had the same right, that the Church had treated her unjustly in a male-dominated society which could not anyway be avoided and which the Church was under no obligation to change. Nor are we saying that our situation here and now, which carries with it the possibility of ordaining women, exists already everywhere in the world. As a result of the social emancipation of woman, which in practice is only slowly coming to prevail, we are in a period of transition, requiring all to exercise patience in the light of the *terminus a quo* and courage in the light of the *terminus ad quem*. Nor is the question of women priests primarily to be regarded in the light of the woman's personal wishes, her self-understanding, and her self-assertion, but in the light of the needs, necessities, and possibilities of a community which must have a leader. Here too it is a question of relative and not absolute ordination. The priestly office as that of the community leader must be regarded as a function of social service in the Church and thus it is contrary to the nature of this office either to refuse it arbitrarily to a particular individual or to demand it unconditionally, when the congregation see no need for this person to exercise the office.

Naturally, if such basic communities gradually become indispensable—since otherwise in the present situation and in that of the immediate future the institutional Church will shrivel up into a Church without people—the episcopal great Church has the task and duty of stimulating and contributing to their formation and their necessary missionary activity. The episcopal great Church must not regard them suspiciously as a disturbing element in a bureaucratically functioning organization. If the basic community is really genuinely Christian and genuinely alive, the result of a free decision of faith in the midst of a secularized world where Christianity can scarcely be handed on any longer by the power of social tradition, then all ecclesiastical organization is largely at the service of these communities:

they are not means to serve the ends of an ecclesiastical bureaucracy defending and wanting to reproduce itself.

If it is claimed that the basic communities can and may be formed from below in the most varied ways and under certain conditions must then be officially recognized as local Churches by the episcopal great Church, this not to deny that in many—perhaps even in most—cases the basic community of the type necessary tomorrow will emerge from a vigorous further development of existing parishes. For the concept of the basic community does not exclude, even if it does not necessarily, imply the territorial principle of formation. In practice, most of the future basic communities will *also* be territorially determined *to a certain extent*, since nothing can be achieved otherwise; but this again does not mean that the 'territory' of one community must automatically exclude in a purely spatial sense the 'territory' of another. For this reason and because of the lack of suitable personalities to create them, the basic communities as understood here for the most part will have to develop out of the existing parishes under the leadership of their present parish priests (in the older sense of the word), using the material resources and juridical structures already available.

The transformation of existing parishes into living basic communities of course presupposes that the parish priest inaugurating and leading it has the right and the courage to some extent to 'neglect' baptized Christians in his parish who cannot be integrated into the new basic community, and to concentrate more on those who are ready, or can make themselves ready, to share in sustaining it. Of course a basic community should not try to be so intense and efficient as to become a closed sect with members and office-holders only interested in one another. An 'integration' of this kind would be wrong. But even if this danger is avoided, in view of the limited pastoral and missionary resources at the disposal of the parish priest and others involved in such a change, the formation of a living basic community out of a traditional parish will not be possible except by doing without—in practice, if not in principle—a number of people belonging on the parish, if only because they will not want to fulfil the very serious demands which the new community makes on them. No attempt will be made in practice to impose these requirements in a legal form, but the new life-style involved in them will in practice lead some people to dissociate themselves from the parish to a degree greater than formerly when they looked to the parish only for the satisfaction of their wholly private 'religious needs'.

These serious demands are of many kinds, as indeed they must be if a parish is not to be merely an administrative unit of the institutional Church or merely a means of satisfying private religious needs. In such a basic community it will be taken for granted that all have an active part in worship, that each in his own way actively shares in the proclamation of the gospel and makes it effective in the concrete situation, and that there is 'lay-preaching'; a Christian awareness will be established in the community as such; its members as individuals and as families will be responsible for one another, giving practical assistance to each other; the community will carry out its mission beyond its own frontiers, to the Church and to the world. All this must be realized in practice and it also requires social structures with functions, duties, and rights, to which individual members of the community and families adapt themselves in a living faith and thus contribute to the general task. The concrete form for all this has still largely to be sought and discovered with the aid of bold experiments. At the same time the attempt must be made to find a genuine mean, avoiding both sectarian introvertedness on the part of the congregation as such and a watering down of demands on the individual which would lead it to revert to an old-style parish, perhaps with an élite— but not the whole community—having something of the character of a basic community.

Where precisely the golden mean lies between a sect and a purely administrative unit of the institutional Church is still today a difficult and unsolved question. Nor can it by any means always be answered in the same way in individual cases. There can certainly be different types from which an individual need not hesitate to choose freely, at least in a large town or city or if he is sufficiently mobile, just as formerly he might occasionally have found the congregation of a church belonging to a religious order more helpful to his spiritual life and preferred it to his official parish, without being prevented by any legal enactment from doing so. When such basic communities from below are attempted and tested experimentally, certain basic types might slowly emerge, have their structure legally recognized from above, and thus acquire greater stability and provide fruitful examples for other cases.

Once again, it has to be admitted that all this is still very vague and abstract. It is all based on the fundamental understanding that concrete and living Christianity today and particularly tomorrow can no longer be passed on simply by the power of a homogeneous Christian society (examples of which are increasingly scarce), by administration from the top, by religious instruction as part of the compulsory education received by every child, but must be carried into the future through the life and witness of a genuine Christian community living out what Christianity really means. Such basic communities in future will no longer be able simply to cover territorially and socially the whole of a populated area; but if they are both very intensively active and at the same time outward-looking, they will be able to be the bearers of the real missionary power of the Church for the future.

This is not to dispute the fact that there must be vital contacts between the individual basic communities, officially maintained or controlled by the Church: there are considerable tasks which are beyond the resources, personal or institutional, of the individual community as such, and demand the unselfish collaboration of all in what is really a service to each of them; there must be a universal canon law both of the whole Church as such and of the German Church, binding on all but assuring sufficient freedom and individuality to the particular community; the diocese, too, must be appropriately circumscribed and structured, since in the church life, spirit, and freedom, on the one hand, and institutions on the other can and must be mutually determining factors.

It could be very useful if jurists were to give thought in good time to the constitution of these basic communities in regard to civil law (legal association, legal ownership, etc.) and how their relationship to the episcopal great Church might be regulated by civil law and so on, so that the communities both acquire the firmest possible solidity in secular law and are ecclesiastically and theologically 'correct'. For we don't know whether the legal status granted to the Churches by the basic law of the German Federal Republic and by other state-laws will always remain so or whether the secularizing process in society at large will continue. For that reason alone the reflections of lawyers on the status of the basic community in secular society may well be part of an appropriate preparation for the future, looking beyond its present needs, if it is taking shape independently and does not simply mean new life within an existing parish and deriving its legal security from the latter.

4

DEMOCRATIZED CHURCH

Once there are sufficient living and yet stable basic communities formed from below, and it is taken for granted in practice in the Church's consciousness that they maintain the reality of the great Churches and are not merely themselves upheld by the latter—that is, they are not merely organs of the great Church, imposed from above—then all the questions raised under the heading of 'democratizing' of the Church will more or less solve themselves in a practical way. We don't want to indulge here in too much theorizing about these questions. This would be particularly pointless since they cannot be solved simply by maintaining or changing the Church's legal structures, but always require a synthesis involving spirit, love, hope, and humility, which cannot be forced or replaced by either authoritarian or democratic legal norms. We shall only put forward a couple of somewhat arbitrarily chosen observations on this theme.

Obviously there is in the Catholic Church one office which does not derive its authority strictly as such merely from the will of the individual members of the Church. This however is not to prejudge the issue of the appropriate and legal mode of appointing the *holder* of this office. Any office-holder is in legitimate possession of his authority only if he lives in unity and peace with the college of such office-holders and their head, the Pope: the exact nature of this *supreme* office and the desirable way of electing its holder today, corresponding to the present historical and social situation, is not in question here. But, apart from this office, there is really no 'divine' law on the exact form in which someone must be selected in practice and appointed to office in the Church. For the fact that such a person must be accepted into the community and co-opted into the college of bishops with and under the Pope, in order to hold office legitimately, does not mean that the decision for or against admission into the college can be left simply to the whim of its members, without any appropriate rules, nor that the Pope must necessarily himself be responsible by divine right for the act of co-option (or, better, for the appointment of the office-holder). Apart from the moral-theological principle that someone as suitable as possible must be chosen for the office, there really is no 'divine law' over and above the rights of the Pope and the college of bishops already mentioned on the exact form of appointing such an office-holder.

It is however obviously a part of his suitability that an 'acceptance' as positive and as universal as possible on the part of those for whom the office in question is exercised should exist or be foreseeable. This acceptance, taken into account in advance, may perhaps not be a factor in the juridical legitimacy of appointment to office but is certainly one which must be considered in the moral judgement of those who are involved in the election. And finally these things are more important than the question of the validity in strictly legal terms of a particular election. It follows—and this is confirmed by history—that the concrete form of appointment of an office-holder in the Church is very variable and must constantly be adapted to the concrete, human and social situation in which the election must take place.

It is of course not possible here to offer concrete, legal models in the light of which the appointment of a parish priest or bishop might be made today in a way most appropriate to the particular office. There can however be no doubt that the forms of election used in the past in accordance with canon law are now at least partially out-of-date and particularly in Central Europe. It is psychologically understandable that an ecclesiastical bureaucracy (which must certainly exist, so that we are using this expression in its proper and not pejorative sense) should attempt the co-option of a new man as far as possible only from its own resources and in this respect it must be credited with goodwill and considerably more experience than is possessed by the average person in the Church. But this too does not alter in the least the fact that today and in the future, particularly in a Church built up more than formerly from below, there must be a greater collaboration—even though in varying degrees—of those who are affected by the appointment. In the long run it is impossible to make sure of the orthodoxy and loyalty to the Church of such office-holders by restricting their election to a small circle of high-ranking ecclesiastics. The danger—which is perhaps not always merely imaginary—of an infiltration of the Church can and must certainly be averted in some other way, even in a more 'democratic' form of election to office. It is hard to see why at least the priests of the diocese concerned should not co-operate really effectively in the election of their bishop.

A more obvious participation of the laity is required, not only in the appointment of office-holders, but also in other decision-making processes in the life of the Church. In such decisions it must be admitted that the bishop has a personal and inalienable right which is qualitatively different from any existing or conceivable right of other members of the Church to share in discussions, but this does not mean at all that priests and laypeople can never have more than an advisory function in regard to these decisions. Such an assertion cannot really be deduced from the orthodox theology of the episcopal office and it also contradicts the actual practice of the Church throughout all the centuries up to the present time. The pastor should remain a pastor, but this certainly does not mean that he is to treat his flock as if they really were sheep. But if this is not to happen, then there must today also be a right on the part of priests and laypeople to co-operate in varying degrees and in forms appropriate to the matter in hand, in a deliberative and not merely consultative way in the Church's decisions. A requirement of this kind may not *a priori* and in principle be suspected as an attempt to democratize the Church in a way contrary to her nature. We can certainly insist that even a merely consultative vote of priests and laypeople in regard to the bishop and of laypeople in regard to the parish priest with the arguments they put forward in the light of the matter in hand should carry considerable weight and of course cannot be lightly passed over by the higher office-holders. But anyone who opposes a deliberative collaboration should be asked why he does so, although it is not in principle contrary to what is properly the constitutional law of the Church, or why he wants to restrict this collaboration to as few and as trivial questions as possible.

Of course such demands and recommendations should not lead to the inflation of the Church's bureaucratic apparatus or complicate and slow down more than necessarily the processes of decision-making. But for the most part the bureaucratic apparatus as it exists is not in fact less complicated than it would be if these demands and wishes were satisfied. This can be seen, for example, in the slowness of concrete decision-making in Rome, leading in matrimonial and other cases to really inhuman effects.

If the decision-makers in the first instance are those at the lowest possible level and as far as possible those who have to carry out the decisions, the processes of decision-making may come about in a completely 'democratic' and transparent way, without the apparatus becoming more complex than is absolutely unavoidable.

5

SOCIO-CRITICAL CHURCH

If we are to talk about what is the most important thing to be done in the German Church of the future, then obviously the question of the Church's service to the world, the social and socio-critical commitment of the Church in all her members and particular groups, cannot be excluded. It is a question we approach with fear and trembling, if only because there has been so much talk about it since Vatican II and because not a few have the impression that, behind all the talk and the appeals about the world-responsibility of Christians and the Church, there lies a tendency towards 'horizontalism', an attempt to make the Church function as a purely humanitarian institution, perhaps even as a merely secular society of the future. Radically as the nature, task and mission of the Church are distinguished from a humanism concerned only with the present world, nevertheless in the light of the nature of the Church and of Christianity itself this world-responsibility is part of the Church's task.

After the Second Vatican Council this is obvious. Love of God and love of neighbour in the last resort are radically dependent on each other. One is mediated by the other. But if a society has become more mobile than formerly, if for the most varied reasons it can and must be changed in order to provide the individual with the greatest possible scope for justice and freedom, then the task of Christian love of neighbour (and of the virtue of justice implicit in this) can no longer be restricted to private, personal relationships. Love of neighbour in such a society acquires also (not only!) a sociopolitical character, becomes necessarily also the will to a better society; it is not mere feeling, not only a private relationship between individuals, but is aimed at changing social institutions—or it is not what it ought to be. It is so only if it is conceived in all its fullness and in the possibilities and tasks of *all* and if its nature is not obscured as a result of individuals rushing in too quickly: for the individual can realize something of its nature within the limits of his gifts and opportunities only when this love is a task and a force that is 'politic'.

At the same time, one thing must be clear to Christians: man is a sinner and this fact must be taken seriously also today. But, according to the teaching of Vatican II (it is obvious anyway), actual social conditions and institutions are also marked by sin. These too are sinful, at least in the sense in which according to the teaching of the Council of Trent and particularly of the Reformed Churches 'concupiscence' stems from sin, tends to sin, and is the object of our constant struggle as human beings and as Christians. The sinfulness of social conditions is simply the pendant to man's internal, concupiscent and combative situation. Man's internal situation in its disorder, its implacable pluralism, its origin from and inclination to sin, faces us again from our external social situation and is not merely an object of private introspection.

Anyone who simply takes social conditions for granted as good must as a Christian face the question whether he really thinks that man is a sinner, that there is a 'sin of the world', that the world is seated in wickedness; he must ask whether his retreat to a private, inner world, where alone the drama is to be played between the redeeming God of freedom, love and justice, and sinful man, does not corrupt Christianity and the unity of the living and historical person at least as much as the attempt to reduce Christianity to a purely humanitarian and social commitment.

The danger of debasing Christianity by confining the struggle with sin to the wholly private sphere is imminent and menacing for two reasons. On the one hand, the institutional factor because of its coercive power and generality creates a temptation to assume that what in fact exists—because of its universality—is also morally legitimate. On the other hand, in a society which is very immobile for a variety of reasons, not working according to a plan and not changeable by a rational decision, what is morally illegitimate in itself and involved in social institutions marked by sin—even if it is felt to some extent to be illegitimate—in practice is scarcely the object of concrete verdicts and morally necessary changes, simply because little or nothing *can* be changed.

For these two reasons and because consciousness in a great

Church changes only slowly, the members and office-holders of the Church are far from being as radically, sensitively aware as they ought to be in face of the task, imposed by Christian love, of criticizing and changing society. Otherwise the suspicion—not entirely without justification—could never arise that the Church is merely a conservative power, devoted to the defence of things as they are. Because of the power of existing social realities, there is a danger—only too often realized—that clever theologians and officer-holders in the Church may very readily and smartly provide the ideology necessary to justify the existing order, particularly since these theologians and office-holders —whether they are aware of it or not—belong to the privileged groups of such a society and therefore almost instinctively and unreflectingly are already convinced of the goodness of the social institutions before they begin to provide the ideological substructures.

It does not seem to me that there is sufficient concern in the Church about this danger rooted in man's sinfulness, particularly since very general principles on freedom, justice, and the improvement of social conditions with a small dose of criticism, which sticks to generalities, only too easily serve as an alibi for us churchgoing Christians to quieten our conscience; general declarations also by the supreme authority in the Church, which can sometimes be very incisive, are in practice ignored by Christians.

If the word 'revolution' does not make us think at once of bloodshed and violence, which is or can be immoral, but is understood as referring to all those vast social changes which cannot be brought about in an evolutionary way with the aid of the already institutionalized and also really functioning means in a society, and if we think of the unity and close interpenetration of all nations and societies in the modern world, then the contrast between the modern industrial nations and the underdeveloped peoples really amounts to a global revolutionary situation, even though the same cannot be said of our own society in particular. The situation is further complicated by the danger recognized today of the aimless consumer society, environmental pollution and so on. But it cannot be said that churchgoing Christians, even including higher office-holders, take this state of affairs as seriously as it ought to be taken.

We are still invoking too one-sidedly the danger of communism and of a totalitarian and authoritarian socialism and we take too little trouble ourselves to find plans and models which we could offer boldly and practically for a future society which can cope with this contemporary situation.

If Christians take seriously *as* Christians their sociopolitical task and the situations in which this must be mastered, then as individuals or groups they cannot fail to work out ideas for the future or to raise demands which will be rejected by other Christians, appealing to the same ultimate Christian principles and motivations. This sort of thing is inevitable today and was recognized as a possibility also by Vatican II. But when Christians are opposed to Christians in this way there is bound to be a great deal of bitterness. They are fighting one another while appealing to what is for both sides an absolute criterion of living. The struggle easily leads to reciprocal 'moral' accusations. But to attempt to avoid this conflict simply by leaving each other in peace or merely formulating supposedly Christian principles which neither upset nor in themselves help anybody would mean that no genuine sociopolitical commitment on the part of Christians would ever be possible. The absence of conflict would however imply a betrayal of essential tasks now facing Christians.

We must therefore learn now and particularly in the Church of the future to maintain the Church's unity and mutual love even in this bitter struggle. This sort of thing must constantly be freshly learned and practised. We must bring a knowledge of the realities of the situation to bear on our arguments and the latter must be intramundane and in the proper sense of the term sociopolitical. We must not invoke one-sidedly the teaching and practice of the institutional Church, whose neutral attitude would then be obscured. But an internal struggle in the Church in regard to these things, in the name of Christian principles, is simply unavoidable. Conflict arises in the last resort from the fact that any application of theoretical principles to concrete situations must involve some lack of reflection and must come up against things on which no adequate reflection is possible: hence the application of these principles takes different forms and the point at which it has to differ, in spite of all reflection and discussion, cannot be precisely determined.

It is of course not possible here to work out an idea of the concrete form of a future social commitment of Christians, Christian groups and ultimately of the Church's official representatives. Here we shall draw attention only to a very few points, mainly those which often seem to be forgotten in the ordinary life of our Church.

It is clear, but we must insist once again, that the Church, in order to become outwardly more credible, must allow that desire for freedom to become more effective in her internal life. We said something already on this subject under the heading of 'democratization'. The work of the synod for the establishment of a system of appeals to judicial authority points in the same direction.

If we speak of Christians and the Church bringing their efforts to bear on 'the world outside', we are not thinking solely of the kind of spectacular declarations and demonstrations organized by student groups and others. Such efforts are justified in principle, may perhaps be required by a Christian conscience, but in particular involve questions of fact which cannot be discussed here, in the light of which one endeavour can be approved, the other questioned; nor should bishops try to prevent by administrative measures sociopolitical efforts of such groups as student parishes merely because they themselves consider the tendency objectively wrong. A student parish, for example, can certainly commit itself politically (which does not mean party politics) in a particular direction, even though this direction seems to some bishops objectively wayward, as long as the student parish does not proclaim clearly heretical fundamental principles or cease to be a community open to *all* Catholic students who want to live with it. But under these conditions such a community is also worthy of financial support by the institutional Church, even if it seeks a political commitment in a direction other than that of the bishops, without of course wanting to bind every one of its members to it.

As we have said, however, this social commitment is not to be found merely in such declarations and organized efforts. The fact that there are other ways of getting involved becomes clear as soon as we recall how few Christian groups, particularly at the roots, are clearly aware of this responsibility. The question of immigrant workers, for example, stirs only a few parishes or basic groups of the Church's organizations, although we must not overlook some laudable exceptions. There should be a social commitment particularly in the basic communities in the process of formation and in the living parishes to be developed in the same way.

We can have the greatest respect for the German Catholic organization for charitable works, *Caritas*, and its manifold institutions and activities. *Caritas* is certainly something of which the German Church can be proud, just because it makes less noise than quite a number of other organizations which behave as if the Church had hitherto done nothing in the social field. Perhaps we may leave aside the question—which might also be raised—whether such organizations as *Caritas*, unintentionally of course, do not sometimes work to preserve the system when it might be the time to change it, even though changing the system is not its task and even when it is difficult to draw the line between improving—with which *Caritas* can be concerned—and changing the system. But the question may well be raised whether this official, institutionalized *Caritas* does not unintentionally provide individual Christians at the roots with a clear conscience which they ought not to possess. Christians today are only too much inclined to leave to official institutions of Church and state what they should do themselves and what really they alone can do by way of Christian love and the defence of justice and freedom.

Today there is certainly much to be done for people which must be done and can only be done administratively by institutions of Church or state. But as a result of this institutionalization and depersonalization new needs and wants emerge: institutional security also involves compulsion. When someone has received from institutions all he needs materially, all that to which he has a right, which he desires, he still lacks what he needs most of all: the person of the other human being. Here is a social task for the basic communities. This task lies in a unique way between the wholly private sphere and the interpenetration of 'intimate areas' of life on the one hand and that part of social life which can be institutionalized on the other. To mention this task does not mean a retreat to pure feeling, a failure to appreciate or a distrust of specialized institutions and their tasks and achievements. But in such basic communities and in them alone can the presence or absence of what is properly human, of what cannot be departmentalized, be observed, 'controlled', and thus too that singular 'achievement' can be 'organized' in which a person realizes himself for another and does not try to make up for this by handing out material aid.

In Christian basic communities that social commitment is possible which does not appear to be social simply because it cannot be institutionalized in an act which is not related to the person performing it, but which is in fact the decisive social work: without it a person is not liberated by the institutions but would be stifled in them and their perfectionism. In the basic community there is scope for that love of the more distant neighbour which is neither mere spontaneous sympathy nor justice that cannot be institutionalized. Obviously this sort of love of neighbour in the basic communities too must be given concrete, material shape, must take the form of neighbourly help, young families closely and vitally linked with one another and working for one another, assistance given quietly and taken for granted from one individual to another. But it exists only when someone gives himself with the gift and the material aid does not separate one person from the other, but brings them together. Such love is possible only in these basic communities (which can be of very different kinds), because only there can the appropriate aid and personal encounter be one. For here we can really still observe whether human beings and Christians are present as such and what is required from them. People can still face quite concrete demands which hold for one individual, call for his personal action, and cannot be delegated to institutions.

A part of the sociopolitical commitment of Christians, their groups, and the Church, which also involves their institutions, is the duty of helping the Third World. A great deal has in fact been said and written about the problem of development aid. But it is obvious that our Christians and Christian congregations are not at all clearly aware of the fundamental importance of this theme for the Christian conscience. It is more or less the same here as with the problem of environmental pollution. Experts call attention to the problem almost in despair; everyone has heard of it; all say that something must be done and half-heartedly some slight effort is made, in a way that hurts no one; then everything goes on as before, as if nothing had happened.

It is the same with the question of aid to the Third World. This aid would be in accordance with the deepest, even the material interests of the highly industrialized nations; at the same time, whether advantageous or not, it is a matter of Christian love. But far too little is done compared to what ought to be and could be done. We are not going to prove it here with figures and statistics: this has been done often enough. When concrete deeds and not merely abstract principles are required, this aid is a very difficult matter, as everything is difficult where there is a question of larger social groups, of economics, money, law, and of overcoming not merely individual, but also collective egoism with its short-sightedness. Today however, when the history of mankind has become one, when there are no longer any areas historically and socially separated from each other, we should be able to see that we are in a global revolutionary situation (which is not the same as revolution). For the social situation of this one world as a whole is characterized by such massive injustice and material peril for the greater part of mankind that it would be impossible to find any institutions capable of removing these things in an 'evolutionary' way and in accordance with principles recognized on all sides in society.

Christians in this country on the whole have not yet become aware of this situation. They are all right and they are too short-sighted to see their more distant neighbour who is not all right. The will to face the problem of the Third World does not mean merely being ready to make a larger personal contribution to the funds of one of the relief organizations or to grumble a little less as a taxpayer about the amount allotted (small enough in itself) in the state's budget to development aid. For once at least we ought to go beyond all this and enter into a mental and material solidarity with those Christians and non-Christian groups which are working for radical changes in the social and economic structures in their own underdeveloped countries.

It seems to me that in this respect Latin America, for which Christianity and the Church bear a special responsibility, should be of primary concern to us. If we react positively in this way to groups in Latin America who are trying as Christians to bring about far-reaching social changes, we need not be too worried here about the right abstract heading under which to describe what they are wanting to do. Revolution must not be understood either in the style of the French Revolution or of the Russian October Revolution and is certainly not something which always and in every situation is bound to be contrary to the Christian conscience or the Sermon on the Mount. Socialism would be a word to be expunged from the Christian vocabulary only if it were made clear how we are to describe the structures of that society which is clearly and truly distinguished from a capitalism of exploitation and inhuman practices, still to be found in the world and expecting Christians to approve or accept it, simply because we are opposed to atheistic and totalitarian communism.

With all this we have still said almost nothing about the concrete duties and tasks of the Christian in regard to the Third World. We cannot work out any concrete programmes here. Perhaps too whatever we might suggest with some hope of its realization would amount to no more than the proverbial drop in the ocean. But even if this were so, even if in this whole question we had to fear historical necessity and the practical impossibility of really mastering the problem in the future, these circumstances do not dispense the Christian from the duty of providing at least this drop. For instance, every Christian youth group of some size might send—as they do in Innsbruck— every year three or even more school-leavers to work for a year as voluntary helpers in the developing countries; every Christian parish might adopt some particular relief organiza- tion in the developing countries; it might be made easier in a human and not merely economic sense for coloured students to study in our country: these are possibilities which really cannot be called Utopian.

The Christian's sociopolitical commitment inevitably involves the question of his relationship to the concrete political parties. For all the future as we can see it, it must be admitted that Christians and the Church will have to get used to the fact— if they have not already done so—that really practising Chris- tians belong to different political parties. There is of course no doubt that a party programme, in itself and particularly in its practical emphasis, may sometimes be impossible to reconcile with a Christian conscience, even though—as in all cases of moral action—this does not imply any judgement on the subjective state of conscience of a Christian who supports an 'unchristian' party. It cannot however be said that a Catholic cannot vote for a particular party merely because one particular point in its programme or of its political decisions is contrary to Christian norms. For, apart from the fact that we should have to prove that precisely this particular decision was clearly contrary to Christian moral law, there simply are no parties which are purely Christian and whose actual conduct would never create misgivings for a radically Christian conscience.

This thesis is not disproved by the fact that occasionally a particular offence against this Christian conscience is not clearly seen or not seen at all in this light in a party, among ordinary people, even by the Church's office-holders, and therefore the party concerned is regarded without any misgivings by the Church generally. In the light of a Christian conscience membership of a particular party, which necessarily and inevitably consists of historically conditioned, short-sighted human beings who also represent selfish interests, can only be regarded dispassionately always as a question of the lesser evil; on this question Christians will never be agreed and this diversity of opinion is inevitably supported on all sides with a Christian motivation and cannot be forbidden to the individual Christian. We have already mentioned this.

EPILOGUE

EPILOGUE

It is obvious, but it must once again be stated expressly, that practically nothing has been said in this little book on the concrete questions with which the special commissions must deal if they are to set out proposals on which the synod can vote. Nothing has been said on the precise form that 'lay-preaching' should take in a normal congregational service, on the question of the conditions required today for the Church to be able to baptize a child, what is the right age for Confirmation, what is the relationship between private confession and a congregational service of penance. There are no suggestions about how the Church can put into effect an active policy in regard to the mass media. No ideas have been worked out as to how ecumenical work at the roots can be continued in the present situation, whether and how the Catholic Church could grant other Christians access to Holy Communion. No answers have been given to questions of the demarcation of a diocese, of its juridical structures, of the relationship of its organs to each other, of a system of appeals to a judicial authority, of the structure of a parish, of the new forms of organizations in the Church. We have not touched at all on relations between Church and state (schools, church-tax, state support for the Church's social work, etc.). Many other questions could be listed with which the synod could and certainly must deal. So, at the end of this little book, we might wonder whether our reflections were worthwhile or altogether too general to be of service to the Church and the German synod.

There it is however. The very fact that there is such an enormous number of particular questions facing the Church today in theory and practice involves a danger of not being able to see the wood for the trees, that the interested parties and experts in a single question will be blind to the Church's task as a whole, in which alone the particular task can be properly mastered. Here of course we cannot attempt to show by individual examples that the general reflections put forward here are also of importance for the one solution of the particular, concrete questions which is right for the future. Such an evaluation of these reflections must be left to those who are trying to see and to answer these particular questions at the synod or outside it. Even an attempt to look into the future is difficult and inevitably comes up against what is obscure and vague; whatever is discovered is necessarily seen only in its pleasant and consoling aspects. But such a look into the distance is necessary if we are not to be cowards, remaining comfortably stuck in the present and only passively awaiting the future. But this glance into the future can be one of faith and hope.